Reinventing Interactive and Direct Marketing

Leading Experts Show How to Maximize Digital ROI with iDirect and iBranding Imperatives

With an Introduction by

Stan Rapp, Chairman, Engauge

New York   Chicago   San Francisco   Lisbon   London
Madrid   Mexico City   Milan   New Delhi
San Juan   Seoul   Singapore   Sydney   Toronto

1 2 3 4 5 6 7 8 9 0   DOC/DOC 0 1 3 2 1 0 9

ISBN 978-0-07-163802-9
MHID   0-07-163802-4

McGraw-Hill books are available at special quantity discounts to use as premiums and sales promotions, or for use in corporate training programs. To contact a representative please e-mail us at bulksales@mcgraw-hill.com.

This book is printed on recycled, acid-free paper.

Library of Congress Cataloging-in-Publication Data
Reinventing interactive and direct marketing : leading experts show how to maximize digital ROI with iDirect and iBranding imperatives / by Stan Rapp.
   p. cm.
ISBN 978-0-07-163802-9 (alk. paper)
1. Interactive marketing.   2. Direct marketing.   3. Branding (Marketing)
I. Rapp, Stan.
HF5415.1264.R45 2010
658.8'72—dc22
                                                                2009026007

For Liz and Stephen, without whose support,
encouragement, and engagement this book would not exist.

Other Stan Rapp Titles

Contents

Foreword

We hear a crescendo of outcries from media and advertising pundits telling us that the sky is falling. Year after year at the American Association of Advertising Agencies (4As) annual convention a litany of agency leaders mourn the loss of the status quo. With the clients' newfound ability to explore marketing directly in low-cost digital media, big agencies are seeing their rich love affair with big media and big money crumble.

What do you do when the reach and awareness of mass advertising are no longer the holy grail? Where do you turn when chief marketing officers (CMOs) no longer settle for vague assurances concerning their companies' ability to measure success? How do you respond when spending is trimmed to weather an economic storm?

But where the mainstream sees disruption and crisis, there are always a few leaders who see transformation and fresh opportunities for growth on the horizon. And that is what *Reinventing Interactive and Direct Marketing* is about.

The day I met Stan Rapp, when he visited me at the ad agency I led, was the start of a dream come true. Together with direct marketing guru Janet Rubio and digital pioneer Jeff Hilimire, we created Engauge, a new marketing solutions agency. We are determined to pioneer innovative collaborative models for fusing data-driven insights and brilliant brand creativity with the interactive dynamo unleashed by broadband connections. The results we have seen for both our business-to-consumer (B-to-C) and business-to-business (B-to-B) clients, tell us we are on the right path.

We have honed this strategy into a pair of singular agency disciplines—**iDirect** and **iBranding**. Both approaches rely heavily on digital technology to achieve the best possible outcome for clients at surprisingly low cost. But this book is not about Engauge. It is an industrywide effort, including a number of our competitors, and is spearheaded by the Direct Marketing Association (DMA). We at Engauge are proud to be the sponsor of publishing *Reinventing Interactive and Direct Marketing*. For the first time, thought leaders from across the full spectrum of direct, interactive, and branding have come together in one place to assess the current scene and, more importantly, to point out what lies ahead. We invited a stellar lineup of contributors with a wide range of expertise to help you get ahead of the curve. Richard Cross, coauthor of *Customer Bonding*,* confronts some of the more perplexing realities marketers face in today's muddled advertising and marketing transition from one era to another. (Chapter 2). Cross provides irreverent, iconoclastic guidance to contend with a marketplace in which twenty-something technology vendors teach veteran marketers the difference between what's right and what's wrong today.

You'll be fascinated by what Michael McCathren, who holds the title of conversation catalyst at Chick-fil-A, has to say about his famous brand and also his unique view of what he sees as the consumer's own **iBrand**—an individual's Internet personal connections with its own positioning and brand equity. (Chapter 12). Your future success as a marketer in the digital era may hang on

*Cross, Richard and Janet Smith, *Customer Bonding: Pathway to Lasting Customer Loyalty*, (New York, NY: NTC/Contemporary Publishing Company, 1996).

how your brand interfaces with what makes your most influential customers' **iBranding** tick.

You can check out the arrival of iDTV—Lucas Donat's model for the next generation of direct-response TV advertising. Donat opens your eyes to a grand new **iDirect** secret of success called iDTV. (Chapter 4). His agency's new-age commercials generate an emotional bond while building a direct-response bridge for the prospect to cross from TV screen to computer screen. In this chapter, Donat breathes new life into the clout of the 30-second commercial.

In Mike Caccavale's entry on how to optimize each prospect and customer engagement, (Chapter 5) you'll gain an appreciation of how the digital revolution has taken data analytics into the stratosphere. You will hear from Professor Don Schultz (Chapter 3) on media budget allocation, and from Joseph Jaffe and Greg Verdino (Chapter10) on how **iDirect** marketers can thrive in the Twitter-YouTube-Facebook era. Dr. Melissa Read speaks up for the use of psychology to drive desired consumer behavior (Chapter 8). Janet Rubio provides an inside view of how B-to-B marketing know-how created a Best Buy for Business data mart to affect sales force performance. (Chapter 11).

You'll read about the demystification of Search Engine Marketing and Search Engine Optimization mastery. (Chapter 6). You'll unravel the complexity of Mobile Marketing in an extra-long chapter written by rising star Michael Becker. (Chapter 7). Mobile, as practiced with an **iDirect** mindset, has the potential to be the most personal, ubiquitous, and measurable marketing channel to emerge in this century. The Internet's longstanding romance with the e-mail channel is highlighted by Jeanniey Mullen, coauthor of *Email Marketing: An Hour a Day*. She shows how to get the most out of what, too often, is given the least attention in the marketing plan—the only media channel where potential customers opt in and invite you to have a close relationship with them. (Chapter 9). And, setting the stage for all that follows, is the opening chapter by John Greco, president of the Direct Marketing Association and leading spokesperson for the new direct marketing of the digital era. Be prepared to set aside any preconception you have about the role direct marketing plays in the twenty-first century. John, in his inimitable forthright fashion, shows how the new direct marketing moves prospects from first interest to closing the sale with cross-channel, digitally driven initiatives.

If any one person deserves a medal of honor for bringing this book to life it is my associate, Stan Rapp, who first conceived the **iDirect Marketing** concept and was then encouraged by John Greco to serve as editor of this anthology. Stan brought to the book's Introduction and his task as editor a lifetime of experience as an acclaimed, six-time author and marketing thought leader. Suffice it to say that few, if any, marketing practitioners today match his past management over a 30-year period of two global advertising agencies that now report a billion dollars in combined revenues. I don't dare say that Stan is a legend in his own time because he brushes off any reference to "legendary" in the media. Legends live in the past. He sees himself very much as living in the present as chairman of our Engauge agency.

Stan's continuing active role as direct marketing's most ardent emissary and visionary over two generations is a model for generations to come. We hope you enjoy and profit from this journey with Stan and the book's contributors into the bright marketing future waiting to be explored today. We are grateful to have lent a hand in its creation.

Rick Milenthal
CEO, Engauge
rmilenthal@engauge.com

What Is
iDirect Marketing?

iDirect is the future of marketing. It's the growth engine at the heart of acquiring and retaining customers in the digital era. Built on a framework of proven direct marketing addressability, it utilizes an abundance of digital tools for engagement with prospects or customers at the time and place of their choosing.

iDirect Marketing reflects a fundamental truth of today's marketplace: Direct is Digital. Digital is Direct. What has been mistakenly viewed as separate disciplines to the detriment of both actually is one and the same. **iDirect Marketing** is interactive, information-driven, insightful, innovative, individualized, iterative. It is grounded in what the Internet and the professional practice of direct marketing make possible.

Both business-to-business and business-to-consumer marketers employ **iDirect** technology to talk to and interact with their customers online. Every company today, in one way or another, is an **iDirect** marketer. It is the most affordable and accountable way to win over brand believers and exceed your revenue goals.

To sum up, **iDirect Marketing** is the confluence of Digital and Direct to drive customer engagement at lowered expense and greater return on investment than ever before. It enhances the value of your marketing database and your ability to generate outcomes constantly impoved by trial-and-error testing.

iDirect marketers go directly to known contacts with an awareness of each person's digital lifestyle to create beneficial online relationships that spread from person to person in achieving accountable, desired sales results.

Introduction

Stan Rapp

Chairman, Engauge

"To face tomorrow with the thought of using the methods of yesterday is to envision life at a standstill. To keep ahead, each one of us, no matter what our task, must search for new and better methods—for even that which we now do well must be done better tomorrow."

JAMES F. BELL, A LEAD SCIENTIST FOR THE MARS EXPLORATION ROVERS

The overwhelming reality of our time is not how much is changing—it is the extraordinary pace of change itself. It seems only yesterday that broadband connections opened a new phase of the digital revolution. Suddenly there were hundreds of millions of people on the planet sharing their lives on Facebook. Just two years after launch, Twitter became a *Time* magazine cover story. Connecting on social networks became the new fascination of marketers.

As the Great Recession intensified, it took about 60 days to say good-bye to the decade's booming economy. And all the while marketers were mastering the new technologies of the digital era in a race to find new solutions at a demanding time to be in business. We saw a reinvented direct marketing with an Internet rocket booster attached lifting advertising and marketing.to new heights of effectiveness.

This book introduces a new paradigm–**iDirect Marketing**–the twenty-first century growth engine crafted at the intersection of digital technologies and direct marketing practices. **iDirect Marketing** is interactive, information-driven, individualized, insightful, iterative and is grounded in what the Internet makes possible as never before. **iDirect Marketing** is today's most responsive, affordable, and accountable approach to attracting brand believers and exceeding your revenue goals.

Along with **iDirect**, this book introduces the **iBranding** concept. Building brand equity in the digital era moves from the TV screen to the computer screen. Advertising is no longer for securing favorable brand positioning in the mind of the consumer. It is also for obtaining a response that takes the consumer by the hand and leads her to a memorable **iBranding** experience online. The insights provided by the marketing luminaries who contributed to this book will open your eyes to astonishing, new opportunities.

The use of digital tools by people in every walk of life continues to grow exponentially. Your prospects and customers stay a step ahead of you by linking up online. They make buying decisions while largely ignoring the bombardment of TV commercials and the relentless assault of advertising messages everywhere they turn. More time is spent in front of the computer screen these days than in watching TV. It's a drastic change that is setting off alarm bells in Madison Avenue offices and in corporate board rooms.

Charlene Li and Josh Bernoff in their bestseller *Groundswell* were among the first to grasp the extent of changed consumer behavior. They told us: "If you have a brand, you're under threat. Your customers have always had an idea about what your brand signifies . . . now they're talking to each other about that idea. They are redefining for themselves the brand you spent millions of dollars, or hundreds of millions of dollars, creating."

What is most alarming about the threat described in *Groundswell* is the denial that takes place year after year at the 4As and the Association of National Advertisers annual conferences. Attendees listen to famous-name speakers (the insiders from an advertising culture that fails to get it) talk about the need for change without offering viable answers. We hear much about the deteriorating state of today's marketing scene. We hear very little from the emerging insurgents who are piecing together a startling new view of marketing that is going to endanger the "prisoner of the past" incumbents significantly. The incumbent agency/media complex frets about its own future while offering hollow reassurance to clients in search of a better future of their own.

What is never mentioned is the full scope of the transformation. Mass media and their companion mass marketing are no more. All those ANA conference attendees are now direct marketers who win market share by marketing directly to build and maintain customer relationships online.

The interface of interactive engagement and direct measurement (an **iDirect** mindset) has replaced yesterday's reliance on arms-length marketing guesswork. Net citizens (two billion worldwide and counting) are masters at ignoring one-way advertising messages. They also are masters at clicking into conversations with a mounting group of friends, extended family, and welcoming strangers to arrive at shopping decisions.

Michael McCathren of Chick-fil-A, offers a seminal revelation in the entry he wrote for this book, (Chapter 12). Marketers are no longer the sole owners of brands. The consumer pecking away at the computer keyboard takes over ownership of his or her personal Internet **iBrand** with its own distinctive set of self-defining components. McCathren tells us that the shortest route to building your business lies in adding value to the customer's **iBrand**.

You may be wondering, "How do I make sense of it all?" So many changes in customer behavior on the Web, new media channels popping up as old media disappear, vocal consumers calling the shots on their PCs and cell phones. It's a change so vast that you need a team of thought leaders to lend a helping hand. No one person has all the answers. No one book has *the answer*.

With the expertise between the covers of this book, you can discover new **iDirect** strategies for spending less to sell more. You learn from academic and info-tech leaders as well as from spokespersons on the agency and marketer's side. This is not a how-to book—even though there is much practical guidance—but rather it is a way to explore promising new vistas that are opening up in the digital era.

LETTING GO AND GRABBING HOLD

Reinventing Interactive and Direct Marketing introduces a new direction in advertising, promotion, and marketing strategy.

The opening chapter is penned by the visionary leader of the Direct Marketing Association (DMA), John Greco. John spotlights what it means to market directly across all media channels regardless of a company's mode of distribution. It's must reading for any CMO who mistakenly confuses direct marketing with direct mail or a few direct response sharpshooters. It's also for anyone who wants to understand direct marketing's new pivotal role at the heart of today's marketing process.

Executives who came to maturity with marketers in absolute control of their brand message still resist accepting the fundamental truths of a new Internet-centric, interactive communication model.

*Every marketer now is an **iDirect** marketer.*

You may be a packaged goods marketer selling your branded products at retail; you may be a brick-and-mortar retailer; you may be an e-commerce merchant; you may be a big-box mammoth with virtual and real world sales channels; you may be a financial services resource; you may be a beleaguered automotive marketer or a flush health-care provider. You may be a B-to-C or B-to-B business. Guess what? All of you share a common need. It is an interactive outpost on the Web where you tune in to what customers are saying and create your own give-and-take community of brand believers. It is also where you respond to another fundamental truth of the new marketing era.

Direct is Interactive.
Interactive is Direct.

What have been falsely viewed as separate disciplines to the detriment of both actually are one and the same. This view is forcefully expressed by Professor Don Schultz in his entry covering media allocation in a consumer-run marketplace (Chapter 3). Dr. Schultz writes about the latest transformation in the long history of direct marketing: "Streaming video, music downloads, consumer ratings of product quality and customer service became commonplace. Social media such as YouTube, MySpace, and now the latest incantation, Twitter, quickly followed. All allow individuals to create, join in, or contribute to their own individually created communities—communities in which the marketer may or may not be invited. The transformation essentially reinvents the isolated interactive and direct marketing disciplines to form a new **iDirect** and **iBranding** configuration."

REINVENTING AD AGENCIES FOR THE DIGITAL ERA

The search for a new advertising agency model made to order for the changed advertising landscape is much in the news. Maurice Saatchi is quoted in *Advertising Age* as saying: "Sometimes I feel as though I am standing at the graveside of a well-loved friend called advertising. Advertising holding companies used to boast about their share of the advertising market. Now they are proud of how much of their business is not in advertising." The CEO of Publicis, Maurice Lévy, was quoted in *Advertising Age* as saying: "It's time to invent the blueprint of the agency of the future. It's not about cosmetic changes, it's about profound and unsettling change."

Only time will tell which of the many moves now underway will provide the ultimate answer—or two or three ultimate answers. While waiting for an agency model truly tuned to the new digital era, most brand advertisers remained addicted to switching from one underperforming ad agency to another equally underperforming agency. Soon, out rolled the much-ballyhooed new big-budget TV campaign. The intended effect seldom materialized. So, two or three years later, there was another round of costly, time-consuming musical chairs. With all the talk about change, very little changed in the agency world until the devastating impact of the Great Recession arrived. Suddenly, accountability was the new buzz word.

My expectation is that the agency of the future will be quite different from those of the past. For one thing, the love affair with the integrated agency model, thankfully, is over. Integrated advertising campaigns are fine. Integrated agencies are another matter. Nobody is good at everything. The whole is less than the sum of its parts. The brand advertising agency integrator almost always calls the shots. The vaunted level playing field is a fiction.

We need fundamental change in what has become a dysfunctional industry. In the **iDirect Marketing** and **iBranding** future, agencies that begin and end their planning with creative use of the Internet experience move to the forefront. Agencies that make a last ditch stand for their creative fixation on the 30-second commercial fade from the scene.

The most valued agency skills now become interactive engagement with the consumer, analytic prowess with the flood of data generated, potent insights gained from toe-to-toe relationships, and all the data monetization schemes that build customer lifetime value for the client. The agency of the future will merge what the "interactives" and the direct response pros do into a singular ability to deliver accountable and **iDirect** results. It will also have a creative **iBranding** capability that makes emotional connections with the target audience to establish and build brand identity online and offline.

Advertising, as a dominant force in marketing, belongs to the twentieth century. The shift to a focus on data-driven, relevant customer engagement in the Internet Age has antiquated the very term "advertising agency." What we are now witnessing is the birth of the *"i-vertising agency."* It is where what happens on the Internet is the centerpiece of agency strategic planning not serving up still more advertising messages people love to avoid.

The **iDirect** practitioners within the i-vertising agency are skilled at tracking both short-term and long-term effectiveness in connecting with old and new customers, interacting with them and maximizing their lifetime value.

The other concentration of talent would be the **iBranding** group. Here we have the strategists and cross-channel creative types adept at moving people to action with brand-building strategies and transformational advertising campaigns. They are masters at reenergizing tired brands, introducing new brands, and helping leading brands stay on top of mind.

This dual functionality model respects the differing skills needed to fulfill very different objectives. It allows each side of the agency team to focus on its own passionate approach to what it does best while joining forces when it is in the client's best interest to do so. It allows for budgeting dollars to go where they can be most effective in getting whatever the client needs done at any given moment.

Some of this is already happening. According to a report in *Advertising Age*, billion-dollar packaged goods advertiser Kellogg found that its use of digital trounced TV by an ROI factor of over 2 to 1. As a result, Kellogg decided to spend more money online and less on TV. Chief marketing officer Mark Baynes expressed the view that maybe the biggest opportunity over time is driven by what the digital environment affords. The ability it provides for improved targeting, engagement and dialogue creates many new opportunities for investment.

NIKE MAKES THE TURN TO iDIRECT AND iBRANDING

Whatever name the new *anyone-to-everyone* marketing may finally go by, it is attracting a host of innovators. You will meet some of them in the following chapters. I'll single out just one—Nike— here. Why Nike? Because it is among the most admired brand advertisers of the past mass media advertising era and was one of the early converts to the tech-driven **iDirect Marketing** approach.

In March of 2007, Nike's CEO boldly announced to the world that the basis for marketing at his remarkable company was about to change. Few of us realized at the time just how fast and how far that change would go. Nike was about to break with its TV-dominated "Just do it" past. Rather than deal with prospects and customers at a worshipful distance, Nike shifted ad dollars to invest in engagement technology that produced some of the most dramatic online activity seen anywhere on the World Wide Web.

One of the **iDirect** building blocks of Nike's new marketing mantra can be found at www.nikeplus.com. It is a joint venture with Apple that gives iPod owners the ability to monitor performance when out on a run with a sensor in the Nike footwear. How well you are doing can be viewed and stored online. Rather than lose a direct relationship after the sale is made, Nike uses **iDirect** involvement with NikePlus to become an invaluable participant in the customer's life as a runner.

In what way might you follow a similar strategy to brighten your customer's life after making a sale?

Another marvel of **iDirect** thinking is NIKEiD. You can go online to customize the look of your running shoe and put it in your virtual shopping cart for home delivery. NIKEiD goes all the way to completing the sale online with direct e-commerce marketing. Nike's pioneering shift from what worked so well in an earlier day to what works so well today is an inspiration for anyone still hesitant to jump onto the **iDirect** and **iBranding** bandwagon. By 2015 advertising and marketing are going to look much more like Nike's new way of doing things than what they did so well before the digital era arrived.

CHANGING TIMES DEMAND A CHANGE IN THE ORGANIZATION

Media changed. Human behavior changed. Shopping experience changed. Social networking never stops changing. So maybe it's time to make changes in the marketing department as well. Are the familiar advertising manager, product manager, information technology (IT) manager, and other longstanding positions really enough to cover what's needed now that **iDirect Marketing** is moving front and center?

Michael McCathren holds a newly created Chick-fil-A position as the company's conversation catalyst. It was just a few years ago that another of our contributors, Joseph Jaffe, published his second book, *Join the Conversation*. I expect we will be seeing many more conversation catalysts following in Michael's footsteps to be sure an authentic brand voice is heard online.

At Engauge, the title of "chief insights officer" was created for Janet Rubio, another one of the contributors to *Reinventing Interactive and Direct Marketing*. It's difficult to imagine any position of greater importance in the modern-day advertising agency. Both on the **iDirect** and **iBranding** side of the shop, sound strategic planning begins with customer insights, business insights, category insights, brand insights, competitive insights, and media insights. Fail to get it right, and you're doomed to failure before you've begun.

My nomination for yet another new addition to marketing management is the CKU (chief keeper-upper). You may be smiling, but the position is not a joke. Being first to grab hold of the latest information and digital technologies is today's great differentiator in gaining marketing supremacy. It is a life or death matter for your business to have someone spotting the latest breakthroughs, meeting with entrepreneurial vendors who are blazing new trails, and evaluating the many alternatives breaking out all over the marketing landscape.

Keeping up with what happened in Argentina is what inspired the decision to create this book. About a year ago my good friend from Buenos Aires, Salvador Filiba, sent an e-mail asking me to write the prologue to a manual being put together by the AMDIA (Argentine Direct and Interactive Marketing Association). I was pleased to take on the assignment. What surprised me was a change in the association's name—what I had known previously as the AMDA (no "interactive") was now the AMDIA.

So, I asked, why the change? Salvador explained that, as far back as 2002, thought leaders in Argentina convinced the association that interactive and direct were one and the same. They believed not only that these specialists should work closely together but also that to advance their capabilities they needed to be within a single association. When it came to realizing how much was changing, marketers in Argentina were far ahead of most of us in North America, Europe, and Asia.

The AMDIA's *Manuel de Marketing Directo e Interactivo* was the first manual in Latin America (and possibly the world) to bring together direct and interactive best practices in a single book. Doing the prologue got me thinking about whether we could create a volume bringing together interactive and direct marketing by U.S. experts for English-speaking marketers. My thanks go out to Salvador Filiba and the AMDIA for planting the seeds of this book. In addition, the thought leaders who generously contributed their knowledge and insights to this anthology deserve a round of applause as well. Despite the 24/7 demands on their time, they put together a testament to the new marketing that a single author could never accomplish.

At every step of the journey in working closely with the DMA to explore the new frontiers of marketing, the support of Sue Geramian has been indispensable. Sue's good cheer and good counsel kept the ship afloat and moving in the right direction. At McGraw-Hill, my publisher's editor Donya Dickerson and her team made it possible to meet an almost impossible manuscript turnaround deadline.

Much of what you will discover in the chapters that follow is not necessarily from your own business category. Surprisingly, this can work in your favor. Starting outside the box most familiar to you often leads to breakthrough ideas you can apply to your own situation. Just ask yourself: "In what way might I take what worked in this particular instance and force-fit it to my own situation?" It's a one-step brainstorming aid that works wonders in stimulating big ideas.

As difficult to accept as the fierce pace of change in marketing today is the absence of certainty that once surrounded what we know and do. At a time when we gave up certainty about the number of planets circling the sun (good-bye, Pluto, it was nice knowing you), adjustment to the changed advertising and marketing universe is also possible. Advertising as we have known it is gone.

Now comes the birth of *i-vertising* driven by a new generation of "creatives." This new, better than ever, accountable advertising is as focused on a powerful "call to action" as it is in forming an emotional connection with the viewer.

It's a new day. The faceless consumer has become your "friend" on Facebook. You can take the pulse of your brand on Twitter a dozen times a day. You can repurpose your TV advertising to create the kind of iDTV commercials Lucas Donat describes in Chapter 4 to lure consumers into a love affair with your brand online. It's a great time to be an **iDirect Marketing** and **iBranding** pacesetter. Everything you need in order to make it happen is here in the pages of this book. Go for it.

Stan Rapp
Chairman, Engauge

As David Ogilvy put it so well in his Introduction to *Ogilvy on Advertising*, I am grateful to my agency associates for supporting my involvement in producing this anthology and "add that the views expressed in these pages do not necessarily reflect the collegial opinions of the agency which employs me."

You can follow me on twitter.com/stanrapp to track the evolution of **iDirect** and **iBranding** as these new disciplines continue to develop in the future.

Chapter
1

Time for Marketing to Really Get Direct about Creating Value

John Greco

President and CEO, Direct Marketing Association

Today, we find ourselves living in a world that's changing in profound ways. The same thing is absolutely true in marketing. Even before all the current economic challenges facing us began, marketing was already in the throes of a paradigm shift that had been steadily gaining steam for several years. Now the enormous impact of macroeconomic changes and market restructuring has accelerated this changeover, intensifying its effect.

In this transition, marketing dollars are shifting from general advertising to measured direct marketing practices. Brand advertising has moved away from one-way, mass media in favor of two-way, one-to-one interactive marketing. Marketing managers are being held increasingly accountable for results, and organizations are making higher and higher demands for obtaining measurable return on investment.

Advances in data processing, list compilation, and digital asset management are feeding this appetite for accountability. As a result, much of today's advertising carries at least one direct response option. All types of marketers are applying new digital technology to begin a conversation with prospects and customers—they're "marketing directly" both online and offline to create data-informed, one-to-one relationships with customers, donors, and prospects.

At the same time, consumers are increasingly comfortable in their new and evolving role as citizens of the constantly expanding multichannel universe. They increasingly live, work, and play through multimodal, multimedia experiences, enabled by the emergence of apparently limitless networking and bandwidth. Successful marketers recognize that today's consumers have an unprecedented range of choices available in both their personal and professional lives for receiving information and making buying decisions. Readers and viewers ultimately make a decision about media, mode, and channel—whenever they choose to engage with a marketer—online or offline, on paper or on screen, at home, at work, or anywhere else.

The primary function of marketing at its heart is to create value for both buyer and seller in any transaction, purchase, donation, or query. This is an ever-changing process, and victory in marketing is accorded to those who do the best job of keeping up with and responding to the changing requirements of consumer preferences and internal accountability. This is the time for marketing pros to seize the moment by really getting direct—truly putting to work all the interactivity and intelligence pervasive in what direct marketing offers.

We have tremendous possibilities right now for accomplishing this change and to really move ahead with ideas and actions that marketers have only talked about for years. This will not be easy. It requires melding the knowledge and discipline of the direct marketing process with breakthroughs in digital interactivity, data gathering, and analytic capabilities. The value we can create by marketing directly will far outweigh the time and cost that go into the effort.

We know from many years of experience that the traditional direct marketing tools of addressability, personalization, direct response, relationship building, testing, and measurement constitute an approach that can be effectively applied across all communication channels. The direct marketing process can be used to add value in many different channels, from direct mail to e-mail, from postcards to catalogs and Web sites, from text messages to online video, social networks, mobile services, addressable cable, and beyond. Beginning with the original non-face-to-face, interactive communications channel—postal mail—direct marketing has morphed as it has moved along, first to the telephone, then to the personal computer, and now on to the mobile device and the set-top box. Today we have a multichannel interfacing world, and marketing must be fluent and facile in all the ways to market directly, from the multidimensional mail stream to the digital bit stream.

At a macroeconomic level the direct marketing process is huge, adding incremental final demand of nearly 10 percent of the entire U.S. gross domestic product (GDP). Direct marketing campaigns in all channels drive well over $2 trillion worth of annual sales. Sales driven by Internet and e-mail direct marketing have grown very quickly over the past few years and now exceed $500 billion. At the same time, the mail channel is driving a total of more than $700 billion in sales—including nearly $155 billion in catalog sales. Telephone marketing delivers more

than $360 billion in additional sales, and direct response adver-
tising in newspapers, on television, and in other media drive more
than $450 billion. Even under difficult economic conditions,
direct marketing–driven sales continue to grow at a pace that's
faster than the overall B-to-C and B-to-B sales growth rate.

This advantage represents an enormous opportunity for direct
marketing—and the people who know how to make it work effectively. This is also precisely why more than 52 percent of all advertising spending now goes into direct marketing channels—over
$176 billion in 2008. Direct mail campaigns and catalogs make
up more than $56 billion of that amount, with growth rates in the
low single digits. Much higher growth rates are associated with e-
mail and Internet marketing, which last year attracted more than
$24 billion of ad spending.

Even with the cuts in traditional advertising budgets made in
the downturn, we fully expect to continue seeing increases in key
direct channels. Growth is likely to be spectacular in the newest
direct channels: social networks and addressable cable. Direct
marketers will continue to use data and analytics across every one
of these new marketing channels and traditional channels alike,
online and offline, to hone customer relationships in ever more
precise measurable levels of value.

Marketing directly is the most powerful force in lifting return
on investment (ROI). How do we know? Here at the Direct
Marketing Association (DMA), we keep a close watch on the sales
driven by direct marketing campaigns and the spending that goes
into them. Across all channels, every dollar spent in 2008 on direct
marketing advertising returned $11.63 of incremental sales on
average. Commercial e-mail produces a return of $45, while
Internet marketing returns almost $20. Direct mail commands
more than $15 in returns. On average, direct marketing advertis-
ing returns more than twice the average for nondirect general
advertising. More than anything else, this fact explains the shift

of advertising dollars to direct marketing. Recently, tough conditions have increased the pace of this changeover.

Marketers need to ensure the ability to survive and thrive in good times and bad by investing in the latest technology, constantly educating and reeducating staff, and nurturing a mindset that focuses on value. We need to engage customers in a dialogue in order to understand how they use evolving media and learn their personal preferences. We need to be open-minded in every aspect of our approach to the future and to test and evaluate everything we do. We need to learn to do more with less through the use of analytics, targeting, versioning, and variable segmentation, even as we raise response rates in each of the channels. Faced with these complex responsibilities, marketing people need to learn how to constantly reevaluate past practices as they also keep up with the latest consumer-to-consumer, shared information trends.

Marketing must have access to both the infrastructure and the data that allow delivery of relevant, addressable communications of all kinds. We must also maintain an excellent reputation for responsible behavior and respect for each person's time and preferences. We must have continuous learning about the transformation in best practices as well as sharing knowledge and experience with others. Successfully meeting all these challenges, from keeping the channels open and economically viable to enhancing marketing's good reputation, represents a demanding task that no individual entity can accomplish entirely alone.

There's a lot of value to be gained in the cooperation within the marketing community that DMA works to facilitate. Our members represent all the vertical industries, such as financial services, pharmaceuticals and health care, retailers, magazine publishers, travel, hospitality, fast-moving consumer goods, electronics, e-commerce, and so on. They are also the users and providers of every media mode, from traditional channels such as mail, telephone, and direct-response TV to the newer cable, satellite, and mobile platforms. Our members provide the many and varied services, specialties, and technologies that make up the entire direct marketing supply chain, from data compilers and list providers, printers, and mailers to analytic services, search specialists, mobile innovators, word-of-mouth marketers, and digital interactive agencies that tie it all together.

Now the exciting vision of the future described in Stan Rapp's Introduction, embodied in the concepts of **iDirect** and **iBranding**, provides a strong call to action for marketers to think and act differently and thereby succeed in a profoundly changing world. By pursuing these advanced goals, I believe that our direct marketing community is well positioned today to help businesses and nonprofits of all sizes and shapes to grow and recharge the economy. While we don't know exactly what's ahead in the next economic cycle, we believe that what you will find in the following pages of this book will be extremely helpful.

DMA members come together to open up this whole new world of possibilities for integrated marketing strategies that are truly on-demand, driven by the interests and convenience of consumers, business customers, and donors. We foster the use of all the available data in order to create truly personal communications, with relevance that goes far beyond just a greeting or headline to offering an engaging, "sticky" experience for each contact with each customer, donor, or prospect. We're helping protect and enhance brands as they move into the direct marketing process in pursuit of faster, smarter, and more profitable results. We're very much looking forward to building multifaceted *direct* relationships between buyer and seller, enhanced by a panoply of digital tools for driving insightful, interactive, Internet-centered involvement. Online or offline, it's all about building one-to-one relationships with your customers—the most important people in your business life. Enjoy and profit from what you will discover in this remarkable anthology and whatever may lie ahead in your marketing future.

Chapter
2

Perplexing New Realities Marketers Face Today

Richard Cross

CEO, Cross World Network and
Coauthor of *Customer Bonding*

As we approach the second decade of the twenty-first century, marketers are coping with the greatest shift in marketplace fundamentals since the invention of the printing press. Think that's overstating it a bit? Check the newsstand in your town. The familiar printed page of your daily newspaper is disappearing in city after city with the relentless advance of everything digital. No longer do you deal with customers at arms' length. Instead, the customer is more likely to be in your face on your Web site or on a Web publisher's irate blog.

Marketers, and out-of-touch ad agency CEOs, who stayed too long with legacy business models, are yesterday's news on Yahoo

Finance and in *Advertising Age*. Tech-savvy, innovative competitors dominate the business buzz on MSNBC.com. But before you give the pace of change on many fronts credit for upsetting long-held beliefs, take another look. What put an end to the usefulness of the 4As comes down to a single, impactful, precedent-shattering event—the grand opening of the Internet's infinite shared space. In this digital wonderland, buyers and sellers from every nation on every continent have all the square "byteage" needed to populate an endlessly scalable brand-new "content nation" (thank you for the book, John Blossom).

In this shared wild-west space, staking out a claim for your brand succeeds or fails based on your ability to get along famously with the content nation's consumers/citizens. It's an untamed "wacky wishful wilderness," where consumers have an **iBrand** of their own (see Chapter 12) and gain fame and fortune by slamming your brand on YouTube or writing a scathing customer review.

The opening of a free-for-all land rush in cyberspace has spurred a new consumerism. Shoppers increasingly devote their most precious asset—time—to seeking the best deals online. Then, after completing a transaction online or offline, more time is spent helping others do the same with openly shared opinions about products used or services received.

This new consumerism along with new information and communication technologies changes the rules of business competition. In today's fiercely competitive environment, gaining market share is less about bombarding the public with intrusive advertising and more about launching a high-tech breakthrough for holding relevant conversations with people to whom you hope to sell something very soon.

The purpose of this chapter is to shine light into the dark corners of the infinite shared space and all that goes on there. So much once taken for granted is no more, so many new findings need to be digested, and there is so much to relearn. It's no wonder you see so many muddled marketers stumbling about. Take heart. If some days of the week you secretly admit to a degree of bewilderment in sorting out what's worthwhile in the "next thing" and what's worth retaining from the old, you've got lots of company. Short-term bewilderment is a natural human reaction to monumental change.

As you will see, the solution calls for adopting an iconoclastic approach of your own. To appreciate the scope of the challenge all of us face these days, it's useful to take a close look at these three perplexing new realities:

1. Vendors now know best, not the marketers or their agencies.
2. Success begins with understanding the technology, not just in understanding the consumer.
3. Infinite shared cyberspace is where brands prosper, not on TV screens.

VENDORS NOW KNOW BEST, NOT THE MARKETERS OR THEIR AGENCIES

iDirect marketing grows out of the explosive growth in powerful, digital technologies that add value to all the tried-and true direct marketing practices. Fortunately, there are dozens of entrepreneurial vendors ready to help with the next inventive tools aimed at providing a better customer experience, delivering more accurate measurement of performance, tracking every move made on the WEB, providing extraordinary market insights, or gaining some other competitive advantage.

It is the **iDirect** technology vendors who open the door to great leaps forward not dreamed of by the vast majority of marketers focused on gaining marginal improvements. They shun the risky "newest of the new" or are just not aware of what's available at a time when so much is happening so fast. All the more reason to add the capabilities of a chief keeper-upper (CKU) as Stan Rapp suggests in the Introduction to this book.

Today's new digital marketing technologies—the drivers of iDirect Marketing success—almost always require a heavy dose of buyer educaton in the form of white papers, seminars, presentations, experiential blogs, and new forms of Web-based learning. What I hear from the smartest vendors is that it is not uncommon to make product presentations to the CEO, CFO, CMO, and IT brass before a sake is made. They all need to be educated.

In those sessions the potential buyer is learning how the new development can solve fundamental marketing problems. Horizons are being expanded. Entirely new selling strategies can emerge. The vendor now can be the emissary of what will make a startling difference in the outcome. The vendor is no longer just the best-price supplier of a resource. Yes, to some degree, this may have been true in the olden days as well. The difference is that today change is constant. In the new **iDirect** world, automatic reliance on long-established norms doesn't cut it.

Scott Brinker, founder of Ion interactive, best known for its post-click marketing application Live Ball, makes the company's product available with and without creative support. Buyers who take just the software product without the right-brain imaginative execution usually falter because they do not take a whole-brain approach. "Businesses buy our product because they want an easy way to test landing pages," says Brinker. "Our technology does that. But once they start testing, they discover that the limiting factor is not the existence or absence of technology at all. It is the creativity involved in putting together the program's execution and devising paths to test."

This realization often leads raw technology buyers back to Ion's creative group which develops the landing pages and test matrix based on what has worked for other clients.

"In effect," says Brinker, "vendors like Ion are the new marketing educators. We publish our blogs and white papers to educate prospects." To prove the point, early in 2009 Brinker coauthored with Anna Telerico an authoritative guide to post-click marketing, titled *Honest Seduction: Using Post-Click Marketing to Turn Landing Pages into Game Changers*. Plus, Brinker's personal blog, www.chiefmartec.com, deals with larger issues of marketing automation.

Without doubt, Brinker is an outstanding B-to-B marketing thought leader in a parade of vendors who bring dozens of potent new tools into play for B-to-B and B-to-C marketers month after month to enhance **iDirect** performance.

Mark Desrocher, CEO of Charles River Interactive, a Search Engine Marketing (SEM) and Search Engine Optimization (SEO) vendor located in Boston, MA, and David Hughes, CEO of The Search Agency (Chapter 6) are vendors who—you guessed it—initiate pacesetting SEO and SEM campaigns for clients. Charles River is deeply involved in the daily operations of marketers it serves. "We see the client's performance data before the client does. We also get to see results across clients and industries before anyone else," says Desrocher.

Everything you've been reading in this chapter about the new **iDirect Marketing** discipline has an equally valuable **iBranding** aspect. The Internet now does for branding what the 30-second commercial once had as its exclusive territory. Desrocher gives the example of a pharmaceutical client marketing its hypertension drug using pay-per-click ads. Preliminary keyword research revealed that consumers search the term "high blood pressure" far more than the term "hypertension." As a result the client was persuaded to adjust its brand positioning from being a hypertension product to being a high blood pressure product.

Brand marketers may find such a strategic positioning process heretical given the many months and tens of millions of dollars that ordinarily go into protracted research, analytics, and ad campaigns to find just the right connection between the brand and the ultimate marketing target. But keywords are different from the words advertisers choose for building brand awareness. The positioning in ads is based on thoughts advertisers want to put into the minds of customers while keywords are the words people already have in their minds about the brand.

All technology-driven decisions must be approached with caution. But it is important to know that your favorite vendor can also be your favorite educator and is likely to possess knowledge not available elsewhere within your marketing group. Only with a genuine partnering mindset will that knowledge become your own driver of **iDirect Marketing** and **iBranding** solutions with results going far beyond anything imagined before.

SUCCESS BEGINS WITH UNDERSTANDING THE TECHNOLOGY, NOT JUST IN UNDERSTANDING THE CONSUMER

"Know thy customer" has been the marketer's cardinal rule for as far back as you want to go. The reason is clear: A marketer needs to know as much as possible about the consumer for the best chance of making a sale. The direct marketing mantra is based on ferreting out customer information, storing it, segmenting customers based on profiling data, and crafting different messages for different segments to achieve the best possible measurable response.

The enormous increase in the number of customer data points generated by online interactive engagement has raised the bar considerably. Each site visit, each click, and each registration adds identifying customer information. The art of sending customized messages based on recipient characteristics has moved far beyond the usual five to ten groupings by segmented demographic, psychographic, and behavioral data to encompass literally thousands of variable messages. (See Chapter 5: More Sales, Less Cost: Optimizing Each Customer Engagement.)

The **iDirect** marketer's dogged determination to gather data at every customer touch point is admirable, but with so many new automated digital technologies to assimilate, the new mandate for the marketers might well be, "Know thy technology vendors."

Google. BrightWave. RevTrax. Pluris. Red Dot. Pardot. Bronto. Salesforce. Goldmine. LiveBall. Omniture. Rapleaf. Real Branding. Alterian. The list could fill a page. Some offer holistic solutions to solve a number of marketing issues. Others stand alone, preferring to be best in a class by zeroing in on a singular digital opportunity.

What they have in common is their influence on the so-called "marketing funnel." It is wide open at the top to capture as many relatively undifferentiated prospects as possible, and narrow at the bottom—where prospects graduate to being customers. The funneling process starts with Google, Yahoo!, MSN, and other search engines and can continue via an almost entirely automated process all the way to the sale using sophisticated new technologies that came into use in the past 24 months. Results for this process are surprisingly strong given that you can make it happen with little or no prior knowledge of the prospect. Very little, if any, customization based on existing customer profiles is required. Some of the most dearly held beliefs of generations of direct marketers may soon be challenged.

Take Google's way of defining a market and a prospect as an example. One of the first choices to make is the choice of a broad or narrow (highly specific) search. If, for example, you are selling branded luxury pocketbooks, you can buy the key phrase "pocketbooks" and get exposure to everyone looking for pocketbooks. Or, you can go to the other extreme and buy such narrowly defined brand names as Gucci or a luxury retailer such as Neiman Marcus. Google will help inform your choices by projecting anticipated traffic for each term. Even so, it is all guesswork at the beginning; you have no idea which terms will lead to sales and which won't.

If you don't trust your judgment as to which terms will produce the most sales, of course, you can turn to testing to find out. For example, you might determine that the best approach is to create a funnel with a narrow top that looks more like a test tube. Prospects who enter your tube are highly qualified by the keywords you choose and the words used in your AdWords creative—the lesser number of prospects you convert at a very high rate

Bill Black, CEO of Construction Data Company (CDC), a Vero Beach, Florida, based B-2-B publisher, offered this comment about digital marketing technologies: "We started buying keywords based on our 20 years of business experience. We are a sales organization and know our customers very well. Our database of prospects included all our potential customers, or so we thought."

By following the broad search approach with Google, CDC was able to identify a much larger audience of potential customers. But the real coup de grâce came when CDC acquired access to some post-click marketing software. Says Black, "We started pay-per-click by using a version of our home page as our landing page. But when we created new pages based on who we were attracting, our conversion rate quadrupled. It changed the whole equation."

Additional breakthroughs came for the company after tests suggested switching its offer of a free product sample to a full 24-hour trial thus allowing prospects full exposure to the company's database of construction projects. With a full array of automated technology in place, CDC continues to see a rising sales curve.

The primacy of technology has not been lost on brand advertisers although they generally are reluctant players. Famed former *New York Times* advertising columnist Randall Rothenberg recently pointed out on the Interactive Advertising Bureau's blog that in these difficult economic times interactive advertising budgets are the only ones growing.

Rothenberg, on the Interactive Marketing Association Web site, posted the following observation from RG/A chairman, CEO, and chief creative officer Bob Greenberg (by latest count, Greenberg's agency has 130 marketing technologists on staff):

> *There are critical creative needs that didn't exist in the old advertising. . . . Advertising is no longer just about the display ad or the TV commercial or the banner; it's about creating meaningful tools and architecting user experiences.*

Greenberg is right, of course. Before creating any online advertising or interactive experience, one has to understand the technology required to bring the idea to life. Customer knowledge enters the picture later when it's time to calibrate the creative to deliver a relevant, meaningful, added-value message.

Nowadays, I still urge clients to be customer-centric (you risk being tossed out of the consultant's union by not saying "customer-centric" at lease three times a day), but I also say, "Think technology first." We move closer each day to realizing the dream of a fully automated solution. The time will come when the CMO punches a few keys on his **iDirect** dashboard and sets in motion a process that delivers just what the CEO wants on the bottom line for that quarter.

INFINITE SHARED CYBERSPACE IS WHERE BRANDS PROSPER, NOT ON TV SCREENS

Futurist George Gilder predicted in his 1990 book *Life After Television* that the TV screen would be supplanted in the American home by the computer screen. Four years later he said, "Just as digital desktop publishing equipment unleashed thousands of text-publishing companies, so the new video-publishing systems will unleash thousands of new filmmakers." The only thing standing in the way, according to Gilder, was the lack of broadband connections.

He got it exactly right. The tipping point for broadband was that day in 2007 when U.S. households passed the 50 percent connection point. Now there are hundreds of thousands of video makers and 3 billion videos being viewed each month on YouTube. In the past year we have seen a new wave of online TV consumption thanks to Hulu, Fox, and the other networks making TV watching online a convenient choice.

What's more, MySpace can deliver 40 million impressions a day on its home page, more than the most watched weekly shows on any TV broadcast network. The dominant social networking sites are so large that in the past few months they eclipsed e-mail as the primary interactive communication tool.

For marketers, the hundreds of millions attracted to social networking means that the treasured mass market declared "dead" so often is alive and well. But reaching the new online mass market and promoting your brand to it is an entirely new challenge requiring an entirely new **iBranding** mindset. And, as long as the conundrum of seeking a mass market in an intimate one-to-one arena remains unresolved, the big money on Madison Avenue will continue being poured down the TV drain and will continue paying more for less and less.

Instead of being focused on consuming televised entertainment and acquiring the products screened in the commercial breaks, members of the new online mass audience lavish time, not money, on what interests them. Connecting to others on a vast scale has become a fascinating way of life almost overnight. It is treasured so much that "friends" and "followers" (as they are called) act as the new currency of shared digital space. The more you have, the richer your online life. In the process people become their own **iBrands**.

Obviously, these developments offer an incredible, but as yet unrealized, opportunity for marketers. The seller's **iBrand** needs to be out there where people gather, where their hearts and minds are. Joining the conversation as a marketer means learning the new language of true caring and openness, learning to mingle with the right people without limits.

The new, overwhelming reality of "infinite shared space" creates a meeting place of unlimited scalability; the sum of all social networking sites, the so-called blogosphere, product and service rating sites, wiki-based sites, and all the sites generated by marketers who have begun exploring the outer reaches of sharing with friends and strangers who become "friends." Newly formed online advertising networks are destined to fail in their attempt to superimpose an alien advertising model on the Internet's community of communities. Unlike offline mass media, mass participation on the Internet is not fertile ground for mass market advertising; people, not marketers, make it what it is.

Even while Facebook, YouTube, and Twitter battle for supremacy and search for workable advertising-supported business models, pioneering innovators are entering the infinite Internet space for sharing to attract their own followers by the millions.

One such brand is Yelp. This relative newcomer publishes revealing consumer reviews of restaurants, nightlife venues, and retailers. Yelp serves up 2.6 million user-provided, uncensored opinions that have won the trust of visitors to the site. What the Yelp crowd cares about is the bare-bones wisdom contributors accumulate in the real world on a grand scale.

Less than four years after its launch Yelp is attracting almost 10 million unique visitors a month—nearly double the previous year's tally. Its success has much in common with other ratings and user-content-based Web enterprises. What is coming next are added features that will give readers and reviewers an opportunity to socialize and interact with one another. The socialized Web continues expanding exponentially, while marketers watch in awe and then go back to doing what comes easily offline on TV, whether it works or not.

The fundamental difference between branding in the outside world and **iBranding** in the Internet's world of unlimited communities is that online the person opting in, not the brand, is on center stage.

And what a stage it is. Unlike any physical place—even the mightiest sports arena—the infinite shared space is *unbounded*. There is no barrier to entry; the sky is the limit when it comes to how many can view a YouTube video or pass along a provocative "tweet."

One of the easiest, and at times the most treacherous, places to do your writing is the blogosphere where marketers have joined the Internet's most prolific bloggers.

Coca-Cola Conversations is a blog all about Coke collectibles. GM uses blogs on topics ranging from auto design to green technologies to getting out of bankruptcy. Johnson & Johnson uses its blog to bring customers inside the company's operations. Southwest Airlines employees interact with customers through the "Nuts About Southwest" blog. One of the Wells Fargo blogs focuses on the company's history. Another caters to students seeking help with their finances. The possibilities for sharing your company's story by blogging in the *uncharted* Web wilderness are endless.

What you can do to build a popular **iBrand** and interact with hundreds, thousands, or millions of consumer **iBrands** in the "infinite shared space" is *unlimited*. Just about anything is possible. All it takes is lots of imagination and a commitment to spend less while doing more with Internet-centered **iDirect initiatives**.

Unbounded. Uncharted. Unlimited. The defining characteristics of the "infinite shared space" create a dream environment for innovative marketing initiatives. It is a playing field that offers marketers a fresh start and a clean palette for building a caring and daring community that lives and thrives alongside the company's **iBrand**.

There are other perplexing new realities facing B-to-B and B-to-C marketers in addition to what we have just examined. But, if you begin to see the world with new eyes, benefit from the fact that outside vendors often know best, give tech-centric the same importance as of customer-centric and begin diverting a good part of your TV-dominated ad budget to **iDirect** online interactive strategies and to supporting your customer's own **iBrands**, you'll do very well indeed.

What I have outlined here is just the beginning of a new break-the-rules approach to boosting business in the face of perplexing new realities. This is a time when marketers have incredible new tools for moving people in the direction desired. But what marketers have to learn is that in the digital era of one-to-one relationships, people also move marketers in ways never before seen.

Chapter

3

Media Allocation for a Mass Networking Era

Don Schultz, Ph.D.

Professor Emeritus-in-Service of Integrated Marketing
Communication, Northwestern University

Clearly, all forms of marketing and communication are on the cusp of change. Evidence surrounds us. Direct marketing, as it was developed over the past 50 or so years, is being buffeted by the Internet revolution. Rapidly developing online interactive technology has made direct marketing more responsive and relevant while challenging the basic assumptions on which most marketers have relied for generations.[1]

The challenge is not just for traditional direct marketing. It's among all forms of marketing communication. When customers gain marketplace control, things must change across all channels.[2]

This chapter reviews the three transformations of direct marketing, explaining how the shift from direct marketing campaigns, as practiced almost exclusively by direct marketers, to marketing directly by most marketers, may be the key element in the emerging "push-and-pull" marketplace.

THE THREE TRANSFORMATIONS OF DIRECT MARKETING

Direct marketing has just entered its third transformation. At the beginning, there was a very basic process of one buyer and one seller meeting in a central location. The merchandise was on hand, the buyer could inspect and ask questions, and the seller could adapt or adjust terms of the offer. Transactions were immediate and transparent. That basic system still exists as an important marketing channel in many parts of the world.[3]

Direct marketing's first transformation happened as the marketplace became more complex. That transformation was driven by rather crude forms of technology, for example, mass printing and mass transportation which enabled marketing on a previously unprecedented scale. It was typified by the emergence of Sears, Roebuck; Montgomery Ward; and Spiegel catalogs. Customers bought directly from the seller, but through mass distributed promotional materials. It was arm's length, but still a direct seller-to-buyer activity without an intermediary.

The 1970s saw the second transformation. Digital technology, through early-stage business computers and data management systems, enabled marketers to identify and track store-level customer purchases over time through a database. That brought traditional retail and direct closer together than ever. Some retailers became direct-by-mail sellers, such as Neiman Marcus and Barnes & Noble, and some direct marketers became store-located retailers, such as Lands' End and Eddie Bauer. The 1980s and 1990s saw development of longer-term customer relationships through CRM (customer relationship management) and lifetime customer valuations which enabled new methodologies for many marketers.[4, 5]

The third transformation began in the middle 1990s with the move to the Internet and World Wide Web. Driven primarily by consumers using search engines, such as Google and Yahoo!, this "customer in control" paradigm was later enhanced by mobile telephony and Web 2.0. Streaming video, music downloads, and consumer ratings of product quality and customer service as well as other customer-controlled interactions became commonplace. Social media such as YouTube, MySpace, Facebook and now the latest incantation, Twitter, quickly followed. All allow individuals to create, join in, or contribute to their own individually created communities—communities to which the marketer may or may not be invited. Consumers love the power provided by the new technologies, but marketers are finding it difficult to monetize the bewildering speed of change and the relationship of equals being created by these approaches.[6]

This third transformation essentially reinvents the isolated interactive and direct marketing disciplines to form a new **iDirect** and **iBranding** configuration. This new approach harnesses traditional direct marketing's capacity to develop fully accountable data-driven outbound communication and also recognizes the importance and impact of consumer-controlled internal pull systems made possible by an always-on Internet connection. Direct and interactive now merge into a singular marketing practice which enables customers to take an active part in the process, and this causes marketers to reexamine many past beliefs.

The development of **iDirect**, which is increasingly the channel of choice rather than traditional mass media, raises some thorny marketing and communication issues. We've aggregated them under the term: "push-and-pull marketing." These outbound and inbound systems, including both digital and analog forms, are today's new reality and are generally new to most traditional and direct marketers.

THE DEVELOPMENT OF PUSH-AND-PULL MARKETING MODELS

Traditionally, most marketing communication, particularly direct, has relied on an outbound approach. The marketer controlled and directed marketing messages to preselected customers and prospects as shown in the basic media communication model seen in Figure 3.1. That approach has been in use for at least the last 200 years.[7]

In this outbound system, the marketer was always in control, that is, determining the product or service to be sold, the price, the distribution system, and the communication forms distributed to customers and prospects. Using that concept, marketers derived the much-acclaimed 4Ps marketing model—product, price, place, and promotion—a concept that hasn't changed in over 60 years.

The problem with the model is that marketers around the world were taught the same model, given the same tools, and started chasing the same set of customers and prospects in the same way. Today marketers distribute far more marketing messages than consumers can absorb. The marketing communication marketplace has become so cluttered that consumers have erected "communication shields" to limit the marketers' incursions into their lives (see Figure 3.2).

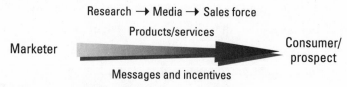

Figure 3.1 Outbound marketing communication model

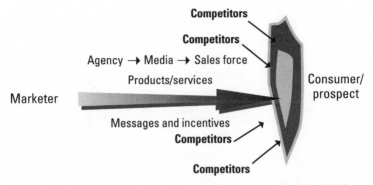

Figure 3.2 Outbound marketing communication model with shield

"Do not call" or "do not contact" lists and more sophisticated tools such as commercial-deleting TiVo are merely symptomatic of the control consumers now use to attempt to keep intrusive marketers out of their lives.

While traditional outbound marketers were busily developing more sophisticated distribution and delivery models to pierce consumer shields, digital technology such as the Internet, the World Wide Web, mobile telephony, and other interactive consumer-controlled systems were developing. These digital systems enable consumers to seek and find information for and about products, services, markets, and marketers in which they are interested, not just what marketers suggest or choose to tell them. Thus we've moved from a strictly outbound to a new individually controlled inbound or "pull" system as shown in Figure 3.3.

Driven by search engines such as Google, Yahoo!, Ask, and others, consumers now can "pull" information from a host of easily accessed sources. They're no longer dependent on the pictures the marketers paint. Consumers can share information with one another and make their own inquiries about what they want and need. It's this customer-controlled pull system that now competes and commonly overwhelms what traditional advertising, sales promotion, public relations, and direct marketers claim about the brand—what the "push" system marketers

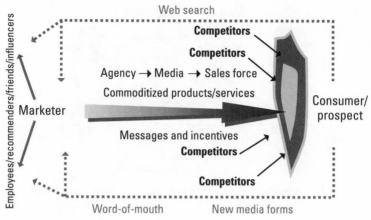

Figure 3.3 Push-and-pull marketplace

have employed for decades. Figure 3.3 illustrates what has happened.

Clearly, today's challenge for marketers is to align and integrate both outbound and inbound communication.[8] Interestingly, both push and pull can be direct channels, but that depends on who is in control of the system. In outbound systems the marketer generally is in control. With inbound systems the consumer controls what is sought or acquired. Thus most traditional media planning, targeting for direct marketing, mass promotional events, and the like become less effective. Muddled marketers struggle to contend with the consumers' ability to select and choose, inquire and ask questions, challenge and refute what marketers say. Most of our traditional marketing concepts, whether they be mass, targeted, or even one to one, are under siege.

What to do?

MEDIA DISTRIBUTION VERSUS MEDIA CONSUMPTION

The challenges facing most marketing communication managers today seem almost overwhelming. New media technologies emerge daily. Old media audiences fragment and disappear. Consumers time shift and multitask. Traditional planning tools such as media cost per thousand reach and frequency share of voice, and other relied-upon techniques are being replaced by click-throughs and behavioral targeting.

With the customer in control, it's time to flip the model around. It's time to begin focusing on gathering media consumption data, that is, learning what media forms customers are using and employing in their own communication systems. It's time to determine how consumers actually are using those media forms, in what combinations, and with what frequency. Then, marketers can be prepared to develop predictive media consumption models as illustrated in Figure 3.4.[9] In short, marketers need to generate input for media planning directly from consumers.

The challenge, of course, is obtaining the data necessary to populate a media consumption model. Fortunately, a new research system has been developed to get that done.

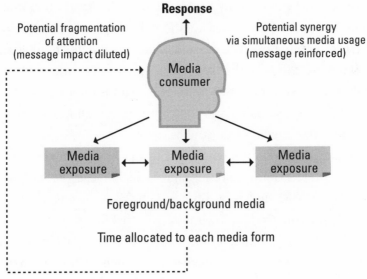

Figure 3.4 A media consumption model

A basic consideration is that today's consumers are "media multi-tasking"—using more than one message input form at the same time. To deal with this, the marketer must know what media forms consumers are using, when they are used, which are being used simultaneously, and so on. To that end, starting in 2002, BIGresearch in Columbus, Ohio, began gathering data on consumer media use. The gathered data sets are called the SIMM studies. The syndicated Simultaneous Media Usage studies provides a tool to understanding the interrelationship of multiple media usage. In October 2002, an *Advertising Age* article[10] introduced the SIMM data to the ad world. The following week Schultz and Pilotta gave the first public presentation of the new technology at the ARF (Advertising Research Foundation) annual conference.

SIMM data are now being gathered twice a year ever since through an online, opt-in process using accepted online-research methodologies. Using a proprietary computer algorithm, incoming responses are sorted by the 14 age–gender cells from the 2000 U.S. census. This approach ensures that each wave of SIMM, generally consisting of 15,000 to 17,000 individual responses, generates a nationally projectable sample of the U.S. population. The current database contains more than 200,000 individual responses. This depth of data allows longitudinal analysis for the first time. The result is information that is much more valuable and insightful than traditional single, point-in-time media usage studies.

In each SIMM study, consumers report on their media usage among 31 media forms, covering online and offline, digital and analog. The SIMM studies by BIGresearch (www.bigresearch.com) provide the data we have used to reveal what forms of media the consumer uses, how much time is spent with each, which media forms are accessed in combination, how much each media form influences various product purchase decisions, what plans there are for product or service purchases in the next six months, and so on. Listings of the consumers' favorite retailer by product category and a host of other relevant marketing and media data become available for analysis.

The extent of basic measures of simultaneous media usage is shown in Table 3.1. To construct this matrix, we took the amount of time consumers reported spending with each media form on an average day (a day = 24 sixty-minute hours, or, 1,440 minutes total). Using this and the reports consumers gave of what media forms they used in what combinations allowed us to construct these types of analyses for the entire market and for various product categories as well.

For example, the combination of television and online, in Table 3.1, shows that, for all product categories, when consumers say they are online, 37.5 percent say they are also watching TV. Alternatively, when the question is reversed, 26.2 percent say they are watching television when they are also online. Clearly, they're doing the same thing each time, but, there's a difference. Consumers are moving some media forms into their "foreground" and pushing others into their "background" range. They're watching TV but monitoring their online system, or they're working

Table 3.1   U.S. Media Combinations
Primary Medium

	Online	TV	Magazine	Newspapers	Direct mail	Cell phone	Radio
Online		26.2	6.1	8.1	9.9	13.9	17.1
TV	37.5		20.2	24.1	21.4	14.9	8.0
Magazines	7.0	10.3				5.0	8.3
Newspapers	10.3	11.6				4.7	11.3
Direct mail	21.0	14.2				6.7	10.7
Radio	21.7	3.8	11.8	12.6	12.2	11.7	

Source: BIGresearch, Inc., first quarter, 2008.

online while television continues in the background. It's this new type of media insight that can change how marketers think about where to put budget dollars.

An example of how consumer media consumption studies can be used to develop media plans for the push-and-pull marketplace follows.

BUILDING PREDICTIVE MODELS

Tracking consumer media consumption clearly enables marketers to develop predictive media models. By knowing what media forms consumers use and how they use them by product category, more efficient media allocation approaches can be developed.

Traditionally, direct marketing has been one of the few communication methods that allows marketers to develop predictive investment and return models. Unfortunately, those models have been limited to the usual direct marketing outbound approaches, that is, direct mail, e-mail, and the like. Developing return on investment (ROI) models becomes extremely difficult to manage, given the ever-widening range of media forms, particularly when the new interactive media are included. SIMM data help solve some of the emerging problems.

The argument for media consumption modeling rather than media distribution modeling is quite simple. If the marketer knows what media form or forms consumers use, how often they use each of them (time allocated), which media forms they use in what combinations and in what product categories, and know which media forms these same consumers say have the most influence on their purchase decisions, fairly accurate predictive media investment models for future allocations can be developed.

Another key element provided by SIMM data is the information respondents provide on their future purchase intentions. SIMM respondents are asked if they plan to purchase a number of major consumer products—automobiles, jewelry, computers, and the like—in the next six months. With six years of data and the law of large numbers available, using SIMM data, we are able to develop predictive media models and align those with customer intent.

The example shown in Table 3.2 has been constructed using June 2008 SIMM data. At that time, approximately 15 percent of the respondents said that they were planning to buy a computer in the next six months. The purchase intent was then combined with media influence to construct the comparison shown in Table 3.2.

The table lists media forms ranked by order of importance, that is, by the influence consumers say the media form has on their purchase decisions for the computer category. As shown, respondents said coupons have the greatest influence in their future computer purchase decision. Next come inserts (Sunday newspaper inserts), then traditional newspapers, followed by television, and

Table 3.2   Purchase Intent and Media Influence
Do you plan to make a computer purchase within the next six months? Yes—84.81%   No—15.19%

	No (%)	Yes (%)	Total (%)
Coupons	26.8	31.0	27.4
Inserts	20.6	25.0	21.3
Newspapers	19.8	24.7	20.5
TV	19.2	26.8	20.3
In-store	18.3	23.3	19.1
Direct	18.2	23.1	18.9
Magazines	15.6	22.7	16.7
Cable	12.3	19.3	13.3
Radio	11.7	18.5	12.7
Internet	10.6	19.3	11.9
E-mail	10.4	16.8	11.4
Yellow pages	6.5	10.5	7.1
Outdoor	6.3	11.0	7.0

so on. Note that only the top 13 of the 31 media forms gathered in the SIMM studies are shown for convenience.

More important than the simple ranking of the media forms are the differences between those planning to buy a computer in the next six months and those who don't intend to make a purchase. The "no" column contains consumers who say they have no intention of purchasing a computer in the next six months. The "yes" column contains those consumers who do plan a computer purchase. It is interesting to note that those planning a purchase have a higher incidence of media usage across the board than those who do not. Clearly, these consumers are in a search mode. Knowing this can help marketers develop the right message for their promotional programs. The "total" column is the average of all those responding to the question in this particular SIMM wave.

Taking the analysis one step further, a CHAID (chi square automatic interaction detector) analysis based on media influence was conducted. CHAID is a well-known direct marketing statistical technique that creates an analytical "tree" by taking the most important initial variable and breaking it down into those elements that created the variable. The algorithm continues the analysis until the pool of variables is exhausted or the output is no longer relevant. The CHAID analysis for the computer category from the SIMM data is shown in Figure 3.5.

As shown in the top box, 14.9 percent of SIMM study respondents planned on buying a computer in the next six months. Media influence factors for these respondents were then grouped into "high," "low," and "no." In this example, the total market can be identified initially by two SIMM respondent groups— those who said that the Internet would have an influence on their computer purchase decision and that the influence would be either high or low. The Internet would have little or no influence on the decision of the third group.

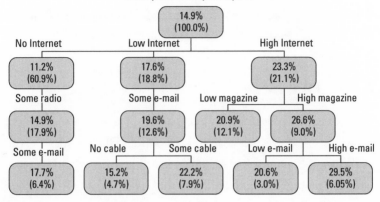

Plan to buy a computer by categories of media influence

Total plan to buy computer

Figure 3.5   Pruned CHAID tree

Taking the analysis to the next level, those who said the Internet would have a high influence on their computer purchase decision can be separated into two groups— those who said that magazines would have a strong influence on their purchase decision (high magazine) and those who said that magazines would have a limited influence, (low magazine). Going to the next step, those who reported a high magazine influence can be further separated into two groups: high e-mail and low e-mail. (Note: The illustrated CHAID tree has been "pruned." That is, not all the interactions and derivatives are diagrammed.)

Looking at the model's output, a marketer can quickly see that the most effective media forms to reach prospective computer purchasers in the next six months would be Internet, magazines, and e-mail. Therefore, marketers should not give cable TV or radio much consideration based on the low influence reported by the SIMM panel.

This simple example illustrates the more sophisticated approaches now available to marketers in allocating their media resources. Developments such as SIMM enable the planner to consider both online and offline, digital and analog, and all the other combinations in the media forms found in the data. In short, this is a new way marketers and their agencies can understand the push-and-pull marketplace of today and tomorrow.

A WAY FORWARD

The challenges posed by the push-and-pull marketplace are just beginning. As consumers gain more control of the interactive conversation, it becomes increasingly clear that **iDirect** and its companion practice, **iBranding**, must make customers a part of the overall marketing program. Marketers no longer can expect to manipulate or even manage customers' behavior. Instead, marketing now becomes a reciprocal process in which marketers and consumers come together to generate mutual benefit. Marketers must provide real value to customers, and customers must share information that enables the marketers to create solutions to fit their needs. This reciprocity really summarizes the push-and-pull marketplace as it emerges and evolves over time. It is only with **iDirect**, a direct marketing mindset that embraces Web 2.0 expertise, that marketers can get the best return for their media budget. But to create that reciprocity, marketers must use new approaches, methodologies, tools, and analytics. Our analysis of the SIMM data suggests:

Knowledge of consumer media consumption and how that consumption occurs is key. This replaces the former thinking that message distribution is more important than how those messages are accessed and consumed at the market level. The media forms to which consumers devote the most time are clearly the ones they consider most important.

The types of media used together and in what combinations are central. No marketer can go forward utilizing only one media form since few consumers limit their media access to a single form. It's critical for marketers to know what media forms consumers are using, singly and simultaneously, and which combinations they most favor.

Media influence is a new way to value media for the push-and-pull marketplace. Only consumers know which media forms they trust and believe in—and, most important, consume. Measured influence can well become the new media currency for the push-and-pull marketer.

Media synergy emerges as a new challenge for marketers, their agencies, and media organizations. Until new ways are adopted to estimate or calculate the synergy among and between media forms, marketing waste will result. This is perhaps the greatest challenge in the push-and-pull marketplace. Finding a solution will result in sizable improvement in return on all marketers' investments.

The arrival of a push-and-pull marketplace opens up tremendous new opportunities for all marketers, particularly those historically involved in direct marketing and for those marketers who now market directly on the Web. If marketers can step back, rethink, and remodel how direct marketing practices can best be wrapped around the incredible customer bonding opportunities offered by the Internet (as the **iDirect** and **iBranding** models set forth in this book demonstrate), we will witness the greatest transformation of marketing effectiveness ever. This success, however, is only going to be what marketers make it.

Notes

1. Schultz, D. E., and H. F. Schultz, *IMC: The Next Generation* (New York: McGraw-Hill, 2004).
2. Schultz, D. E., and M. P. Block, *Media Generations* (Worthington, OH: BIGresearch, 2008).
3. Stone, B., and R. Jacobs, *Successful Direct Marketing Methods*, 8th ed. (Columbus, OH: McGraw-Hill, 2007).
4. Nash, E., *Direct Marketing: Strategy, Planning, Execution*, 4th ed. (Columbus, OH: McGraw-Hill, 2000).
5. Shepard, D., *The New Direct Marketing: How to Implement a Profit-driven Database Marketing Strategy* (Homewood, IL: Business One Irwin 1990).
6. Schultz and Block, *Media Generations*.
7. Sissors, J., and L. Bumba, *Advertising Media Planning*, 5th ed. (Lincolnwood, IL: NTC Publishing, 1996).
8. Schultz, D. E., B. E. Barnes, H. F. Schultz, and M. Azzaro, *Building Customer-Brand Relationships* (Armonk, NY: M.E. Sharpe, 2009).
9. Schultz, D. E., and J. J. Pilotta, "Developing the Foundation for a New Approach to Understanding How Media Advertising Works," paper presented at ESOMAR WAM Conference, Geneva, Switzerland, 2004.
10. Cuneo, Alice, "Simultaneous Media Use Rifle, New Study Finds," *Advertising Age*, October 7, 2002.

Chapter
4

Direct Goes Emotional with New iDTV Advertising

Lucas Donat

CEO, Donat/Wald, a pioneering iDTV agency

"**B**reathe in fresh air with every puff" of a Salem cigarette.

It's hard to believe that in the early days of television there were ads like that one extolling the delights of smoking. If you view it on YouTube, you can understand how an earlier generation came to believe that smoking was good, clean fun.

We've come a long way since then—when most advertising sent its emotional grabber in one direction, from the "creatives" at the agency to the consumer in front of the TV screen. One-way advertising opened the door to a mass marketing era driven by brands connecting to the consumers' emotions with their ever-escalating bombardment of advertising messages. Looking back from a twenty-first century vantage point, that one-way approach feels more like manipulation than a true connection.

In our digital age, it's already obvious that the top-down, one-way approach doesn't fit the online mold where blogs, Facebook, MySpace, Twitter, IM, e-mail (and on and on) enable two-way messaging in real time, and the ability to have user-generated content and opinions broadcast to hundreds, thousands, and even millions of others in mere seconds.

What's not obvious yet is how network and cable TV advertisers will respond now that much of their audience spends more time emotionally involved in front of a computer screen than in front of their TV. Consumers addicted to intense social networking, blogging about a subject dear to the blogger's heart and clicking into a 24-hour news cycle, are resistant to the usual, lackadaisical, emotion-lacking fare served up by so many of today's agency creatives.

Rather than rising to the occasion, Madison Avenue is moving in the opposite direction. In reviewing a bunch of directors' reels recently, I found that few commercials offer a moment of real emotion that drives true interaction between the brand and the viewer. All advertising, no matter the form or function, must embrace emotion to connect with today's always-on consumer. By "connect with" I mean lead directly to actions that generate increased sales. Because all ads—whether they make consumers laugh or cry or something in between—are designed to do one thing: *sell stuff*.

So, when I talk about creating emotional connections in advertising, it's not only because I think it's the right thing to do (which I do). It's because I know it's the smartest, most effective way to sell anything. Emotional engagement improves hearing the message you want delivered. And I have the numbers to prove it.

When I started my ad agency in the mid-1980s, direct response (DR) was the most uncool specialty you could choose. I remember winning our first award for a campaign we produced for 1-800-DENTIST. The trophy was a phone receiver mounted on a stand and spray-painted gold. When the trophy was handed to me, the gold paint literally was still tacky to the touch. It was the perfect metaphor for the industry at the time.

Back in the 1980s, the "brand guys" were the cool ones, the creative "artists." DR people were number crunchers. I couldn't get truly talented creative directors to stoop so low as to work at a direct marketing agency, no matter how much money was offered. They wanted to do the important work, the stuff that built brands, the stuff that won awards at Cannes. And, looking down from their pedestals, any advertising with a visible call to action that was held accountable for motivating a response couldn't possibly build brands.

Direct response then was a medium that relied on generating *an impulse* to buy a gadget or miracle-working appliance or to get someone to sign up for a subscription right now. DR wasn't the realm of brand. It wasn't the realm of higher emotion. It was the realm of base impulse: sex, greed, vanity. The TV commercials or the print media ads relied on a formula that drove to close the sale within the advertisement itself—to get those phones ringing, to "act now."

But that was then.

More recently, both brand and DR have been moving toward the middle. Having experienced a taste of measurability in their online campaigns, brand advertisers increasingly want direct marketing's accountability with their traditional brand advertising as well. Meanwhile, DR stalwarts today know the value of moving beyond flashing toll-free numbers to the value of creating a brand that inspires trust and loyalty. Bringing the best of both together becomes possible with **iDirect**'s recognition of the Internet as the focal point of the twenty-first-century marketing universe.

Today, if you want to connect with the consumer, there's only one place to be—and that's online. Advertising's most important task is to make an emotional connection that takes the consumer by the hand and leads her or him to a relevant, interactive online experience. It's the place where anything and everything is possible for monetizing the relationship. Whether it's a TV commercial or a print ad, if it fails to present clear motivation to visit the advertiser's Web address, at least half of the budgeted expense has been wasted.

The Internet is the most important direct response advertising destination of the digital era. Marketers embracing the **iDirect Marketing** imperatives now can have it both ways. It is possible to create ROI-positive advertising that builds brands while generating accountable results.

The response can be handled offline at a call center or at a Web address that over time completes an e-commerce sale, generates a quality lead for the B-to-B marketer or an in-store coupon for the B-to-C marketer. Forget DRTV! It's time for what Stan Rapp and I call iDTV—one of the key components of the most effective **iDirect** strategies.

The "i" stands for stimulating Internet traffic, involvement, influence, and interactivity.

The "D" stands for direct marketing accountability and lifetime value.

The "TV" stands for—60-second, 30-second, and 15-second TV commercials.

The first rule of iDTV advertising is that the commercial has an offer that drives targeted viewers to an opt-in, data-generating *Internet* experience. The iDTV commercial, with its emphasis on **iBranding** as well as driving response, is for any marketer who wants a direct relationship with end users of their product or service, not only for direct marketers. There is no requirement to drive an immediate transaction as with DRTV, you just need to create *involvement* with the prospect or customer and begin a value-added **iDirect** conversation or activity (see Chapter 10: Conversation: What Matters Most for Marketers Now).

A new tech-savvy generation of creatives stands ready to devise brilliant *interactivity* once you have those opt-in Web addresses. This triad (interest, involvement, interactivity) can set in motion an emotional connection that translates into enhanced lifetime value and brand believers who digitally spread the good word about you.

THE SUPER BOWL TEST LABORATORY

In 2008, a handful of Super Bowl advertisers gave us some great examples of how to use TV to drive viewers to the Web and build lasting connections with potential customers.

Hyundai's two third-quarter iDTV spots drove potential buyers to the marketer's Web site, hyundaigenesis.com. It worked— 300,000 people went to the site during the game, generating 25,000 rich sales leads that the company turned into fresh revenue and new relationships thanks to good use of e-mail interactivity.

- E*Trade's "Talking Baby" ad led to a 32 percent surge in newly opened accounts the week following the Super Bowl. Online searches for the brand grew by 1,000 percent from the hour before the game to the hour after the game.
- Audi, with an iDTV offer, saw its Web traffic climb 200 percent in the 30 days following the game—quite a plus, when over 80 percent of car buyers shop online first.
- CareerBuilder saw a 68 percent jump in job applications in the three months following the game.

Think of it! All those other advertisers who ran the usual Super Bowl hodgepodge of plain old brand advertising with failed emotional connections and no direct response call to action blew away $2.7 million on each spot (over $120 million in all). That's not just my view. Here's what Bob Garfield had to say in *Advertising Age*: "On their biggest day, marketers and agencies fielded a weak team. If this was supposed to represent the best Madison Avenue has to offer, the losers were not confined to the football game." A year later at the 2009 Super Bowl, it was the same story. This time $200 million was thrown away on soon-forgotten (if ever noted) "nonvertising." This is what Stuart Elliott said about it in the *New York Times*: "Americans have been disappointed and appalled by Wall Street banks, investment counselors, Detroit, hedge fund managers, and the governors of at least two states. . . . After Sunday you could add Super Bowl advertising to that lengthening list of letdowns." Why does TV advertising that drives the right people to the right online connection result in sales, as iDTV Super Bowl winners in 2008 and 2009 proved? The answer is in the new reality that your customers lead a digital alternative life

- with friends—on social sites like Facebook, MySpace, and Twitter.
- with shopping—using forums, blogs, search engines, comparison pricing sites, and ratings research based on user experience.
- with brands—via the company's Web site, live chat customer service, online account management, e-mail newsletters, online coupons, rewards programs, and myriad other ways.

The built-in interactivity of the Internet—the ease of creating digital involvement—gives advertisers a chance to form much deeper relationships with customers and potential customers than ever before.

Traditional DRTV is an impulse-driven medium looking to close a sale right then and there. So it requires half-hour and two-minute formats as the mainstay of its creative communication. The new iDTV commercials, on the other hand, allow for a much shorter format of 60 seconds, 30 seconds, 15 seconds, and even 10 seconds. Remember, all we're doing in these ads is generating enough *i*nvolvement to stimulate *i*nteraction on the *I*nternet.

In fact, with the iDTV model, the shorter the format, the higher the efficiency. This isn't to suggest that a brand can be successful with only 10-second spots. Generally it takes a good mix of 30- and 15-second spots, before a 10-second spot will produce. But in time, we have found that iDTV advertisers can enjoy very high efficiency with 15s and even 10s. No longer do we need a half hour or 2 minutes to make advertising pay out in accordance with the DRTV standard.

Because iDTV can make traditional brand advertisers generate ROI positive results, it will also become the new form of brand-building advertising. Creating and enhancing a brand in today's economy starts with building a satisfying, interactive relationship with potential customers online. That relationship can take in much more than, and go far afield from, the attributes of the product or service being sold. One of the best reasons for a marketer to turn to an **iDirect Marketing** strategy and create an **iBrand** is the efficiency and effectiveness of iDTV advertising and iDPM advertising (the direct response print media version).

THE CORE ELEMENT—EMOTION THAT DRIVES REAL CONNECTION

How do you make an emotional connection that will result in a successful interactive relationship that inspires sales? You have to know your customers and know why they buy your products or use your services. The number crunchers get excited here, since they've made it their mission to gather insightful data online and offline about the customer.

But analysis of demographics, spending patterns, even online surfing habits is not the end-all and be-all of success. In the new **iDirect Marketing** paradigm, that analysis falls short when advertisers—yes, even those schooled in the science of DR measurement—keep that data locked in the cerebral left brain, while ignoring the heart-centered right brain.

Stop thinking about customer data as cold numbers or information unrelated to an emotional component. The mortgage industry has no shortage of data on its customers. Neither does the car industry. Or banking. They are awash in data, and yet they missed what the market was telling them. If emotion is what drives brand preference, as marketers have known since the first cigarette ads, then why do we tend to view data through a nonemotional lens?

At the center of the new **iDirect Marketing** described in the Introduction to this book is the left-brain assurance of addressability and accountability wrapped around right-brain insightful intelligence of what is burning in the heart of the consumer. With a trusting emotional connection between marketer and customer, you'll be amazed at what will be disclosed to you online. With that knowledge, the connection you can make on TV, in less than a minute, to future customers doesn't seem quite so daunting or esoteric.

Let's look at two companies that have successfully identified the point at which they can make an authentic emotional connection with potential customers and have used iDTV to drive prospects online and involve them in an interactive relationship.

eHarmony: The Power of Caring

One of the iDTV advertising pioneers is eHarmony, a company that has built its entire brand equity by using the direct response channel while breaking most of the tenets of DRTV.

The company's first DR departure is at the most basic level: its brand promise. It won't make you thinner or richer or sexier. eHarmony promises the very highest prize in the emotional hierarchy—love. As of this writing, an average of 236 people get married *every day* because they met on eHarmony. That's 2 percent of all marriages in a year, in the United States alone. How has eHarmony achieved this level of success? By building a brand that people trust.

eHarmony's founder, Dr. Neil Clark Warren, believed that the company needed to understand people as deeply as possible in order to match them well. So he and his team of researchers developed a 450-question personality profile that probes every aspect of the prospective member's life—from the basics to spirituality to attitudes about sex and money.

Even more amazing, Dr. Warren felt that it was very important to ask prospects to answer all of the 450 questions before even considering taking their money. The exchange of this much personal information between company and customer was unheard of at the time. Who would trust a business enough to answer so many personal questions on a Web site before making a purchase? So far, 20 million people have done it. And it's all been driven by highly emotional iDTV advertising that asks men and women to log onto eHarmony.com and begin the process of completing the detailed questionnaire.

Experts in advertising and online marketing scoffed when Dr. Warren said he wanted to have people answer the 450 questions before finalizing the transaction. "No one is going to answer all those questions. It's too personal, it's too long, and it runs counter to everything we know about placing barriers before checkout." This was the prevailing admonition of the online marketers and the traditional direct marketers at the time.

But guess what. The prognosticators were all wrong. People poured their hearts out in that questionnaire. And they continue to do so by the millions today. Too often, companies pass up an opportunity to involve their customers in an interactive relationship because they fear scaring off potential buyers. But if your advertising and your customer service people have made the right impression, you win trust, and people will tell you almost anything. In fact, they want to do it if, in return, they expect to receive real value. But you have to earn it. And you have to be ready to listen to what people have to say. You have to care, and you have to show that caring attitude in your advertising. Dr. Warren cares deeply about his customers, and everything about the company he created reflects that authentic caring.

There are few things more powerful in life than feeling cared for. And nothing builds greater brand loyalty. Witness the eHarmony commercials. eHarmony has built its brand on the testimonials of real couples that are the embodiment of this kind of brand loyalty. I've had the privilege of working on the advertising for eHarmony since its very first television commercial. As part of our casting process, we ask eHarmony couples to send us home videos telling their eHarmony story. It is impressive to see the lengths to which these wonderful couples will go to film themselves, edit the shoot, add music, and ship the video to eHarmony. Why do they go to all this trouble? Because they felt that eHarmony cared about them and delivered on its brand promise.

By combining the best of brand building with the best of direct response, eHarmony became the number-one most trusted brand in the online dating category. And, because its TV advertising has been ROI-positive, eHarmony was able to out-spend the competition by 2-to-1 in the early days. The ability to profitably reinvest in its advertising, a hallmark of iDTV, was what gave the company its foothold in one of the most fiercely contested categories online. That foothold was quickly parlayed into the position of leadership it enjoys today.

According to an independent study by Rosetta Marketing Strategies, eHarmony became the category leader across virtually every brand metric—trust, reliability, match-up compatibility, scientific process, rigorous screening, and happier marriages.

Lest that sound too touchy-feely, eHarmony brand metrics translates into dollars. In a very short period of time the Internet's most trusted matchmaker commanded more dollars spent in the market than its two largest competitors.

LegalZoom: The Power of Story to Create Emotional Connections

You may be thinking: all well and good for eHarmony, but can the high degree of loyalty and trust achieved by eHarmony apply to an advertiser offering a service with much lower emotional engagement? Yes it can. And here's why: Whether you offer a product or service, online or offline, you are hoping to satisfy an emotional need for someone. Once you identify that need and tap into it, you'll be able to drive potential buyers online and involve them in a relationship with your brand.

If you're not sure about exactly what that need is, just ask. Chances are, there is a link between your product or service and either a positive emotion or a particular problem that is causing anxiety for consumers. Can you ease their fears about a scary economy? Can you make their jobs easier? Can you help them compete against larger, more established businesses? Whatever your actual product or service, it's more than likely that there is an emotional need driving the desire for it.

So here's an example of a company that, on the surface, might seem far from the kind of emotional involvement that a dating site can offer. It's LegalZoom, an e-commerce company that helps people prepare personal and business legal documents, such as wills or business incorporations. Talk about dry and tedious. Legal services has got to be it, right? How could a company in such a dry category build a powerful emotional connection?

LegalZoom helps people save time, money, and hassle on tasks that they probably wish they didn't have to do. Not much excitement there. Dig further to the next layer, and we find that preparing personal and business legal documents can be a costly and frustrating experience for most people. For that reason, according to LegalZoom, nearly 70 percent of Americans do not have a will, and many people who try to complete their own legal documents make mistakes.

So LegalZoom helps people overcome frustration and probably fear, and is helping them avoid what could be costly mistakes. The problem is that people don't want to be reminded about their failings, particularly in advertising. If I don't own a fire extinguisher, I don't want to hear about all the terrible consequences if I don't buy one today. I'd rather avoid the whole subject.

Time to dig deeper. Where is the emotional connection associated with tedious legal matters? People don't just get a will; they protect their families. They don't just obtain a provisional patent, they launch a dream. Protecting a great idea, starting a business— suddenly all these things become possible with the right legal assistance.

That's what the company tapped into for its TV ads. The campaign included four 30-second and 15-second ads, each featuring real stories of people who turned to LegalZoom's online legal document services to achieve a significant milestone in their lives.

"Daddy" is the story of the Bryants from Pasadena, California, who created a will to protect their adorable nine-month-old daughter Chloe. "Fishbait" tells the tale of Leo Croisetiere from Richmond, Virginia, who lost his leg and his ability to launch bait when surf fishing—so he invented a fish-bait launcher. He obtained a provisional patent for his creation through LegalZoom. "Toffee" tells the story of Janet Long from Clayton, California, who turned her mother's beloved toffee recipe into a business—which she incorporated through LegalZoom.

The campaign communicates the heart of what LegalZoom does for people—which is to help them realize their dreams in a way that is easy and affordable. What better way to talk about these services than to tell those stories? By identifying the core emotions that motivate people in need of a legal document, LegalZoom fulfilled a new role in the lives of its customers—from merely providing legal documents to becoming a partner that empowers them to realize their dreams and feel protected while they do.

The brand relationship online is a reflection of what the advertising promises. A visit to the LegalZoom site begins the process of getting your legal ducks in a row. A will is a very intimate document, and requires that customers share personal information. They'll do that only if they believe that LegalZoom is a company that cares about them. The informed involvement that takes place on the Internet does everything imaginable to create a believer in the brand. LegalZoom is a new breed of direct marketer, better described as an **iDirect** and **iBrand** marketer.

The key to connecting with your potential customers is to understand—and tap into—the emotion that lies at the heart of what you're offering to do for them. Every marketer—whether B-to-C or B-to-B—has a story to tell. If your story appeals to the heart and is told from the heart, and with the added discipline of an **iDirect** mindset you have a winner.

The new iDTV approach to television advertising serves a higher purpose than does traditional brand awareness advertising. It makes a memorable, emotional brand connection *and* starts a productive, interactive relationship with responders on the Internet. Marketers who fail to understand that **iDirect** and **iBranding** stategies are the new order of the day are condemned to throw their money away on ill-considered TV ads as surely as those Madison Avenue losers at Super Bowl 2008 and 2009.

The way consumers consume media is changing fast. The way consumers relate to and interact with your brand on the ever-expanding social interface of the Internet is changing even faster. But what never changes is the wonderful ROI of two-way advertising that starts with an authentic human emotional response and ends with profitable involvement and interaction in cyberspace and retail space.

Chapter
5

More Sales, Less Cost: Optimizing Each Consumer Engagement

Michael Caccavale

Founder and CEO, Pluris Marketing

Consumers are reaching out to brands more than ever, yet conversion on direct mail and e-mail campaigns is at an all-time low. What's going on? Are consumers more engaged or less? Why are marketers and consumers not connecting? These challenging questions must be answered in order to move on to the next phase of the **iDirect** revolution.

What's changed, of course, is that today's consumers have rapidly adopted interactive methods of communication that put them more in charge than before—enabling them to explore new ways for getting what they want when they want it. Leading marketers recognize that most of the messages they push are not being absorbed or even noticed, let alone acted on. The onus is now on the marketer to be prepared to meaningfully engage the right consumers and their best customers whenever and wherever they reach out. How? By fundamentally changing the way they apply analytics—from "whom to promote" to "how to engage."

Get it right, and the results can be stunning—ROI gains of over 1,000 percent, conversion gains of 30 to 100 percent. With millions of consumers knocking on their virtual doors every day and immense pressure on ad budgets, marketers have plenty riding on better preparing themselves to optimize the value of each of these interactions.

iDIRECT CHANNELS—A BOOM OR BUST PROPOSITION

Consumers are flocking to interactive channels and avoiding noninteractive ones. In fact, in addition to using the new **iDirect** channels such as blogging, the Web site, chat, and the latest "hot" social media, consumers still like to pick up the phone and talk to a real person.

Case in point: The U.S. call center market continues to thrive at $18 billion in spending on outsourced inbound and outbound sales and service. What's more, these centers have evolved into "contact centers," handling chat sessions, tweets, Web leads, and e-mail contacts, which result in a measurable lift in sales performance because interactivity and immediacy create better customer service and, thereby, help close sales. Through improved sales and service productivity, existing marketers, empowered with consumer data and analytics to sell in a proactive, service-oriented context, are equalizing the labor arbitrage benefits of moving centers offshore.

Network and cable television ad dollars continue to shift to more interactive and measurable channels as ad-skipping and time-shifting practices enabled by digital video recorders (DVRs) proliferate. A staggering 83 percent of 200 top U.S. advertising executives surveyed by the DVR Research Institute sited DVR use as the greatest threat to the effectiveness of TV advertising. New and emerging formats like in-game advertising were named as the second biggest threat. Hulu, a nonlinear distributor of premium video content over the Web, is achieving double the brand and message recall rates on its advertising content compared to cable prime advertising and almost that great a lift over broadcast prime by inviting viewers to decide what advertising content they want to view. Prefer to watch a 3-minute movie trailer and then watch your 22-minute sitcom commercial free? No problem. Want to rate which spots you like or dislike and influence what advertising is offered in the future? No problem. Developing the means to give users more control over their experience is delivering tremendous improvements across every measure of effectiveness.

E-mail is expected to continue to soar and it is expected that the channel will grow to over $15 billion in spending by 2013. But when response rates to e-mail are at an unprecedented low, further (ab)using the channel won't close the gap. In fact, declining e-mail response rates point to the single biggest challenge **iDirect** channels pose to marketers—the boom will go bust if you aren't prepared to engage each consumer in a relevant and meaningful way from the first moment of contact.

Interactivity represents a phenomenal opportunity to connect with consumers and increase value and loyalty right up to the point where an organization is unable to deliver. Similarly, as interactive media become a bigger part of the marketing mix, marketers have to address the risk that many of these media are not matching the quality and lifetime value of customers won with direct mail in the mix. Direct mail consistently produces more repeat purchasers over time, even when purchase typically occurs in other channels. Media like television and direct mail are proven to lift the performance of other media, notably search, e-mail, online and affiliate programs, and contact center volumes. Hence, the imperative for **iDirect** marketers—the key to achieving dramatic ROI gains—is to adopt analytically driven, highly administrable, and relevant ways to engage each consumer from the first moment, thereby paying off media investments with higher conversion and the quality of buyers that produces loyalty over time.

The startling reality is that most brands are not prepared to engage consumers via interactive channels. A Web site making the same offer to everyone or tapping an ad network to monetize remnant inventory is done absent of objectives oriented to consumer value. Complex rules engines that lead to a cascading series of questions to qualify a customer into an offer, whether online or in a contact center, drive up cost and frustration with minimal effect to relevance.

THE PAY-FOR-PERFORMANCE MYTH

Trusting response rate and conversion woes would soon be forgotten, and starry-eyed marketers hailed pay-for-performance as the saving grace for marketing accountability. Now that they only had to pay for "action," marketers reveled in the cost per acquisition (CPA) model, shifting massive spending to online media. Many were equally exhilarated over e-mail marketing because of the very low cost—fractions of pennies per message. Both media solved the ad cost constraint without analytics most people didn't understand.

Now a little hungover from the CPA rush, marketing executives realize that while not paying for non-action-creating impressions is great, what they really need is a consistent, larger, and higher-quality stream of "A's."

Neither e-mail nor CPA programs solved this problem. To the contrary, the hundreds of online ad networks, many of them catering to direct response marketers, are scrambling to find ways to get ad inventory to perform and prop up cost per thousand prices, which declined by more than 50 percent last year, according to the PubMatic AdPrice index.

Unfortunately, some marketers are trying to fight the decline in e-mail response by sending greater volumes of e-mail, most still untargeted and irrelevant. Consequently, 80 percent of the nearly 1 trillion e-mails sent in 2008 went totally ignored. With response rates at an unprecedented low, "list fatigue" is a frequent lament. Further (ab)using the e-mail medium did not deliver more response—not even for bona fide messaging.

Marketers don't need more impressions; they need more actions. It is what lies at the heart of the **iDirect** mantra. Turning to myriad affiliates and ad networks to drive up volume without quality control, they risk losing control of their brand and messaging.

With a more precise engagement strategy, procuring the right impressions and higher conversion, marketers will drive more, higher-quality customers to their brand.

AN ANALYTICAL (R)EVOLUTION

The Root of the Challenge

The challenge in moving marketers' mindsets from "whom to promote" to "how to engage" is rooted in two decades of marketing science aimed at applying analytics to solving one key constraint—advertising cost. With the arrival of a new generation of **iDirect** and **iBranding** marketers, concern with low-cost, effective customer engagement has moved to the forefront of agency and client interest.

In the direct mail world, marketers strove to promote to as many people as possible at a breakeven cost per mail piece of $.50 to $1.00. Marketers built models to determine whom to target in order for them to achieve a certain level of performance, usually resulting in mailing only the first couple of deciles in a model and ignoring everybody else (the other 80 percent).

The stronger a brand, the more consumers will initiate contact with that brand. For environmentally friendly sportswear manufacturer Patagonia, this is exactly the challenge. Over the past three years, the number of visitors to its Web site that can't be tied back to a specific catalog mailing, search term, or e-mail has gone up well over 300 percent. What brought them to the site? How can Patagonia engage them? Should those visitors be part of the small group Patagonia remarkets to with a catalog?

With consumers initiating hundreds of millions of interactions, the constraint has changed. Removing incremental advertising cost means that there is no more plausible excuse for ignoring the other 80 percent, especially not for offers with broad market appeal. It becomes a matter of which offer to present and how to package it for any given consumer to optimize the desired **iDirect** result.

Evolution in Targeting

This evolution of targeting approaches can be summarized in three stages—selection-driven, event-driven, and analytically driven. (See Figure 5.1.) **iDirect** marketers, if anything, are even more concerned about getting the targeting right as their traditional direct marketing counterparts were.

In a selection-driven approach, marketers select a segment of consumers to promote to based on certain criteria and send them all the same offer, mindful of the premise that efficiency and volume lower cost.

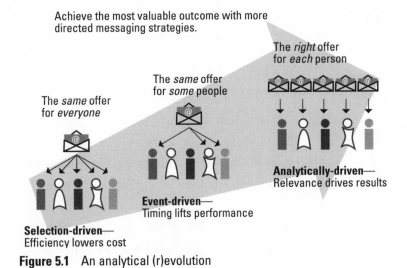

Figure 5.1   An analytical (r)evolution

Event-driven communications are cause-and-effect campaigns. A brand observes certain actions or behaviors and initiates a campaign consistent with the observed event, taking advantage of the close timing and affinity in order to lift results. Event triggers are often based on life events, specific behaviors like a first-time purchase, or any event indicating that a consumer may be in the market for a related product or service.

Improving selection methods and building event-based marketing systems were a primary point of innovation in marketing science through the 1990s and into the twenty-first century.

Evolving still further is the analytically driven approach to consumer engagement—using rich data sources and analytics to predict myriad outcomes to specific marketing objectives and optimally aligning all elements of the offer mix to optimize the value for each person and the brand. As in the case of Hulu, the inclusion of collaborative data captured by giving users more control over their experience makes this approach all the more powerful.

Rather than narrowing a target audience to figure out whom to exclude from a promotion, an analytically driven approach explores how to include all members of an audience, aligning the optimal offer for each individual to effectively hit as many points along the demand curve as possible.

Effectively, we have reversed the offer/audience axis. Before, marketers used to create an offer for promotion to the largest audience possible via the broadest reach media available. Today we personalize the offer mix to create thousands of offers addressable at the individual level and promoted via an interdependent mix of offer and order channels and media to optimize conversion rate across a string of contacts.

This is not an indictment of broad reach media. To the contrary, marketers choosing to blindly scratch television or direct mail from their marketing mix would most likely see a precipitous decline in performance on other marketing investments.

The question *du jour*: What is the right media mix to feed the sales funnel, moving from awareness and consideration to ultimately achieving the highest possible conversion on each consumer engagement?

HOW TO OPTIMIZE EACH CONSUMER ENGAGEMENT

Now that we're versed in historical perspective and theory, let's lay out how to go about optimizing consumer engagements and rewrite ROI expectations.

A well-crafted consumer engagement strategy extends the classic 4Ps of marketing (product, price, place, and promotion) at an individual level while adding contemporary, actionable dimensions to create the optimal offer to each consumer, based on his or her life cycle stage with a brand. The approach can be broken into four phases: data integration, predicting behaviors, determining offers, and engaging the consumer. The primary focus will be on the approach and analytics concerning predicting behav-

More relevant. More effective. More value.

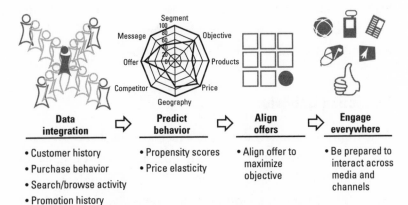

Data integration	Predict behavior	Align offers	Engage everywhere
• Customer history	• Propensity scores	• Align offer to maximize objective	• Be prepared to interact across media and channels
• Purchase behavior	• Price elasticity		
• Search/browse activity			
• Promotion history			

Figure 5.2   Optimizing consumer engagement

ior and aligning offers and messaging at the consumer level. (See Figure 5.2.)

Suddenlink Communications, a top-10 U.S. provider of cable, Internet, and telephony services, serving over 3 million homes in 21 states, implemented such an analytically driven strategy to optimize how it engages consumers in the contact center and on the Web. The company's objective was to create a more consistent sales and service process, improving the quality and consistency of customer service representatives' (CSRs) performances, while improving their sell-through rates in the call center and on the Web by no less than 20 percent.

Consumer Data Integration

Clearly, a well-crafted consumer engagement strategy is data-enabled, the performance only as good as the data that feed it. The first building block is to mobilize consumer data, including promotion, purchase, and service history, and link it via a unique personal identifier. For Suddenlink, that entailed sourcing data from multiple internal operating and billing systems. The company was able to enhance its view of the individual customer with several third-party data sources to improve the predictive quality of the data. Sources of interest often include demographics, psychographics, compiled purchase and preference data, and online search and browse activity.

Predicting Behavior

Analytically determining the right elements of the offer mix for any given consumer requires predicting outcomes across a range of dependant variables from which products or combinations of products a consumer is most likely to purchase to the individual price elasticity of each consumer, consumers' ability to pay, and their receptivity to competitive offers. Applying the insights from these models to construct offers, one element of the offer mix at a time, and varying the elements for geographic and competitive market factors as well as creative and messaging appropriate for each consumer segment results in a very large catalog of available offers. (See Figure 5.3.)

In the case of Suddenlink, a company with three core products, that offer catalog quickly grows upwards of a thousand different

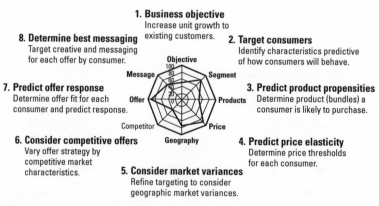

Predicting outcomes enables optimization.

1. Business objective
Increase unit growth to
existing customers.

8. Determine best messaging
Target creative and messaging
for each offer by consumer.

2. Target consumers
Identify characteristics predictive
of how consumers will behave.

7. Predict offer response
Determine offer fit for each
consumer and predict response.

3. Predict product propensities
Determine product (bundles) a
consumer is likely to purchase.

6. Consider competitive offers
Vary offer strategy by
competitive market
characteristics.

4. Predict price elasticity
Determine price thresholds
for each consumer.

5. Consider market variances
Refine targeting to consider
geographic market variances.

Figure 5.3   Analytically driven offer mix

offers. For some brands this could grow to several thousand offer derivatives to manage. Traditional selection-driven methods of selecting an audience for each of those campaigns would quickly bog down.

Optimizing and Aligning Offers

While using analytics to predict behavior is essential to the science behind offer construction, it is equally important to aligning the optimal offer, over all other available "in-market" offers, ahead of each individual's next interaction with the brand.

The consumer life cycle serves as a timeless and incredibly effective grounding point during offer construction, and more so when aligning offers. Acquisition offers vary greatly from those geared toward the development, migration, and retention of current customers or "win back" of those terminating their service.

Changes in the overriding business objective (for example, switching from maximizing unit growth to optimizing profitability) will require a realignment of appropriate offers.

Just as algorithms looked across all the propensity scores of a consumer to determine how to best bundle a given product, algorithms must look across propensity scores for each resulting offer to determine the appropriate offer for each consumer based on the business objective at play. Using analytics and automation is the only plausible way to manage many thousands of offers, creative style variations, and messaging options across millions of consumer interactions, supported by thousands of frontline sales and service staff people and multiple other interactive channels.

Engaging the Consumer Everywhere

This trailblazing form of marketing enablement requires exceptionally agile data and analytics platforms that procure the right offer and messaging the moment a customer, or some identifier linked to the customer, is identified—on the Web, phone, or otherwise.

At Suddenlink, upon identifying the consumer, a Web-services call is made from that touch point to the offer and content management database, retrieving the optimal offer prepared for that consumer. In fractions of seconds that engagement is supported by rich consumer information and analytics. By delivering the offer and supporting information for each offer in a consistent way, a CSR is able to comfortably represent 20 times more offers, greatly improving their effectiveness. In the case of Suddenlink, the resulting gain in conversion was 34 percent over control groups, realizing an annualized value of $7 million on the first program alone. Free of incremental marketing cost or added call handling time, Suddenlink achieved a stunning 1,600 percent ROI.

These results directly translated to the Web as well, where instead of serving up largely the same offer for each million site visits, Suddenlink served over 230 different offers per million visits, increasing sell-through by 24 percent.

Every day optimization analytics are reprocessed, taking that day's results and promotion history into consideration. For instance, if consumers making a service call one day accept an upgrade to their service package, we don't want to offer it to them again the next day on the Web, especially not at a different price point. A simple "thank you for your order" and confirming their install date for next week is a much better approach.

BE PREPARED

It's definitively proven to be true that an **iDirect** approach with more ways available to relevantly engage a consumer, the more value we will create. In fact, marketers are seeing gains in conversion accelerate as they have more well-crafted offers in market.

The finer the grain of our targeting of offers to the consumer, the more points along the demand curve we are hitting and the more precisely we are able to refine our messaging.

Advances in database and networking technology and the application of advanced analytics have set the stage for the unique **iBranding** and **iDirect** era of enhanced growth in marketing productivity. Be prepared. The Boy Scouts had it right after all.

Chapter
6

SEM and SEO: Core Drivers of iDirect Success

David Hughes

CEO, The Search Agency

Search engine marketing (SEM) and search engine optimization (SEO) are cornerstones of the **iDirect** approach. Each practice began as a somewhat mysterious combination of technology and trickery, and the average marketer at first either could not understand it or could not gauge its value.

Search has since evolved into one of the most measurable forms of direct marketing and is the foundation of any online marketing effort. For any business—small or large, B-2-B or B-2-C, whatever distribution method used—showing up on the first page of the major search engines for a broad set of queries can lead to exponential increases in awareness, demand, and revenue growth.

SEM, also known as paid search or pay-per-click (PPC), consists of sponsored textual advertisements that appear above or to the right of the organic search results. SEO is a systematic process of altering a Web site's architecture, content, and internal/external links to get optimally indexed and ranked in the organic search results. Most marketers understand the basics and have already incorporated both of these channels into their direct marketing efforts.

Soon after launching a full-scale search marketing effort, it is easy to get overwhelmed by the amount of data and number of keywords that need to be managed. The complete transparency and up-to-the-minute results of a paid search campaign or an organic traffic report are both a blessing and a curse.

In real time and on an ongoing basis, advertisers can test and adjust all aspects of their campaigns—from keywords, to creative, to bidding strategy, to landing pages and conversion paths—to improve performance and control budgets. However, without a coherent framework for managing this volume of information, marketers often end up in an endless cycle of changing ads, adjusting bid caps, creating new landing pages, and rewriting Web pages without any clue as to what's working and what's not.

SEARCH ENGINE MARKETING: A PERFORMANCE MARKETER'S DREAM

In a perfect **iDirect** world, marketers would be able to connect every dollar earned to every dollar spent. Each strategy and tactic would be evaluated in isolation, and an accurate return on investment would be determined in real time. For most organizations, however, reaching this point requires an entirely new approach to handling data.

Back in the early days of paid search, measuring the effectiveness of a campaign required the ability to connect the amount one spent on a paid search advertisement to the corresponding conversion metrics (sales, leads, etc.). As the practice evolved, many online businesses discovered that optimizing campaigns to a static metric is not an accurate measure of campaign performance.

For example, a cable television provider would be willing to pay a higher cost per click to obtain a customer that subscribed for two years than for one who cancelled after six months. Insurance brokers would be willing to increase their cost per acquisition if they could predict which of their online leads would be eligible for a higher-margin policy. For most online businesses, optimizing a campaign based on gross conversions will never be as efficient as optimizing based on the *value* of those conversions as measured in revenue, net margin, or lifetime customer value.

New SEM tracking technology enables performance-driven marketers to capture these more robust conversion metrics. Also, incorporating cost of goods sold data with optimizing based on net margin has resulted in marked improvements for a number of e-retailers. Through the use of tracking pixels or cookies, a business can now account for most latent (delayed) conversions and improve results based on the projected lifetime value of a customer. When you include these more robust and relevant conversion metrics in your bid methodology, incremental spend can be allocated to those keywords and advertisements that yield the highest ROI.

Whether your company is just starting out with SEM or has been running multi-million dollar campaigns, there are some fundamental **iDirect** strategies that can enable you to more accurately measure effectiveness and drive continued growth from this vital digital advertising channel:

1. *Comprehensive integrated data.* Having end-to-end visibility into your paid search campaign performance is

the foundation of any superior effort. The objective should be to create a single reporting platform for connecting data from the search engines with data from your internal accounting systems and your bid optimization platform. By mapping click traffic data with detailed conversion data, you can allocate incremental spend to those campaigns that yield the greatest ROI.

2. *Efficient account structure.* Managing an ever-increasing collection of keywords is one of the biggest headaches of SEM. Customers use all types of terms when searching for your product, and the list only increases over time. In order to manage your account most effectively, keywords should be bucketed into narrowly defined groups around a common theme, product, type of customer, or stage of the buying cycle. Tightly constructed ad groupings enable you to serve highly targeted ads and landing pages to distinct customer segments. The results lead to higher conversion rates and improved keyword quality score.[1]

3. *Targeted creative.* Writing paid search advertisements may seem relatively straightforward since search engines such as Google allow only 25 characters of text in the headline and two rows of 35 characters each. However, with such a small amount of on-page real estate and no opportunity for branded elements or logos, presenting a targeted, relevant offer alongside the search listing becomes even more critical. The creative should be clearly stated, ideally include words from the original search query, promote your value proposition, and specify your competitive differentiators (all in 95 total characters!). The offer should be compelling and include a very direct call to action. For example, a photo-sharing offer should end the ad with,

"Submit your photo now!" rather than the more generic "Click here."

4. *ROI-based bid management.* Paid search is an auction, and figuring out how much you are willing to bid on an individual keyword is a crucial and dynamic function. At any moment, competitors are increasing or decreasing their bids, and the search engines are reshuffling the order in which ads appear as well as how much each click-through will cost. Knowing the "right" bid for any given keyword or campaign presupposes you know your key metrics or business objectives. If your goal is to drive sales volume or revenue, you may be willing to spend a bit more on certain keywords. If your objective is to manage your campaigns to very narrow cost per acquisition (CPA) goals or return on ad spend (ROAS) metric, you may sacrifice some volume, but will gain in efficiency.

5. *Optimized landing pages.* Most of the discussion of paid search focuses on preclick decisions—determining which keywords make sense for your business, writing effective ad copy, and calculating how much to bid on each keyword or campaign. Along with these tactics, optimizing the user's *postclick* experience can drive game-changing improvements in SEM. A well-designed landing page should be relevant to the keyword query and should reiterate the promise made in your paid search advertisement. It should minimize the path to conversion and eliminate any roadblocks for the user. An effective landing page or microsite will reduce your bounce rate, boost quality score, and increase your overall conversion rate and total revenue.

6. *Test, measure, test, measure, ad infinitum.* SEM is the ultimate channel for data-driven decision making.

Every aspect of a campaign—from the keywords chosen, to the ad copy, to the maximum bid, to the landing pages, to the search engines, time of day, day of week, and geography—can be modified and its impact measured. No other advertising channel offers such a wealth of targeting options with such a robust and timely means of tracking performance. Indeed, what makes SEM such an intriguing and challenging medium is that no campaign ever reaches the perfection stage—results can always be improved, and the search engine technology has made it relatively easy to tweak each element and measure its discrete impact on performance. Continuous testing is the mantra of any successful SEM **iDirect** effort. Very likely, SEM is the ultimate example of how the arrival of Internet-based intelligence took the longstanding direct marketing practice of constant testing to heights no person could have imagined a generation ago.

SEM CASE STUDY: REAL ESTATE DEVELOPER

The following case study provides a representative example of how a traditional offline business utilized an **iDirect** marketing approach, driven by paid search to more than double its online leads generated monthly and reduce CPA by more than 200 percent.

SEM Marketer

The advertiser is a national developer of high-end apartment communities. The company manages 80 apartment communities and attracts online traffic to a corporate Web site which provides information about each of its properties. There are detailed overviews of over 50,000 units, with the latest listings and promotions.

Challenge

As paid search campaigns became increasingly successful, the company struggled to manage the growing number of keywords within an individual, fixed monthly budget for each apartment community.

Solution

The company reorganized all keywords into smaller campaigns organized by geography and customer stage of the buying cycle. It then implemented more advanced SEM tactics to increase total conversions and reduce CPA:

- *Running national campaigns with geo-modified keywords.* Many of the company's most critical keywords such as "apartments" or "apartments for rent" were very expensive because of their popularity. And they were difficult to convert. Rather than draining its budget on these high-volume terms, the company tried running narrower campaigns on geo-modified keywords (e.g., San Francisco apartments). This strategy provided exposure to local residents and apartment seekers looking to move to a new city.
- *Day-parting.* The major search engines allow advertisers to decide exactly when their advertisements will run. The apartment community developer management examined its conversion data and found that the highest-converting traffic came during regular business hours. By increasing its maximum bids with allocation of most of its budget from 8 a.m.–6 p.m. in each time zone, it was able to capture more of this premium Web traffic and increase total conversions.

- *Expanding keywords and ad groups.* After a few months of running these campaigns, the advertiser could identify the high-performing keywords and ad groups. The company tried a wide range of tactics including misspellings, synonyms, and abbreviations for those campaigns and obtained high conversion rates with the available budget. The total number of keywords under management grew by 64 percent in the first 12 months, but the inclusion of new keywords was based on actual performance, rather than brainstorming wild ideas.
- *Connecting ad copy to the latest promotions.* Based on a rigorous testing methodology, the company identified a core set of descriptions and calls to action that yielded a consistently high level of conversions. It was able to drive even higher conversion rates by spelling out specific, time-sensitive promotions for each of the properties and then directing the Web searcher to a targeted landing page that reiterated the special promotion shown in the advertisement.

Results

In the first 16 months of the enhanced campaign, the company more than doubled its number of online leads per month and reduced its CPA by more than 200 percent.

These best practices can apply to any business looking to advertise online. Some online businesses invest millions of dollars in paid searches. Other companies have much smaller budgets. Some make it a small part of their marketing mix; others use paid search as their only form of advertising. Regardless of the size of the company or level of SEM spend, applying a systematic, data-driven, and iterative approach to SEM will invariably produce measurable improvements on your key metrics. Getting SEM right ranks in importance for today's **iDirect** marketers at the same level as getting the creative right in a 30-second commercial ranked for yesterday's mass marketers.

SEARCH ENGINE OPTIMIZATION: A THREE-TIERED APPROACH

Since the mid-1990s, SEO has developed from a somewhat mysterious collection of Web-development strategies and ethically questionable tactics into an ROI-driven, indispensible, and often underappreciated fundamental of any online marketing plan.

As the practice matured, a wide range of best practices and how-to manuals became available to assist Web masters in getting optimally indexed and ranked results when customers search for their brands, business category, products, benefits, location, and other related keywords. SEO is composed of three areas of distinct expertise: architecture, content, and linking.

- *Architecture.* Providing an efficient site structure to allow the search engines to find and assess the content of your site. This includes having clean internal links and an accurate site map accessible from all pages.
- *Content.* Once a search engine reaches a page on your site, it reviews the URL, title tags, headlines, and on-page content to determine the most relevant subject or keywords. Understanding how to optimize the content of each page for a given keyword leads to improved rankings.
- *Linking.* Search engines also measure the number and quality of external and internal links to each page. Search engines view external links as a "vote of confidence" for the specific pages. Links from outside sites deemed to be an authority on your subject matter are

given more weight than links from unrelated or less authoritative sites.

In order to develop a sustainable competitive advantage through SEO, marketers must gain unique insight into site performance and customer search behavior and adopt an analytics-based approach to project prioritization. It's also necessary to follow a flawless implementation process on executing site updates and responding to shifts in the marketplace. What follows is a step-by-step plan to guide you in moving from tactical execution toward strategic enhancements that will have longlasting effects on organic listings.

Campaign Planning

Performance-based **iDirect** marketers begin by conducting a thorough analysis of their Web site, customer behavior, business objectives, and competitive environment. From this analysis, they develop a comprehensive list of keywords and segment them into narrowly defined "keyword campaigns."

The groups of similarly themed keywords are analogous to the ad groups that have become the hallmark of admired paid search marketing. Brand terms are managed separately from product terms. High-performing category keywords are separated from more granular long-tail words. Bucketing keywords into tightly defined campaigns enables efficient prioritization and measurement of results.

Opportunity Analysis

Each keyword campaign is then connected to a new or existing Web page targeted toward a specific customer segment or stage of the buying cycle. Campaigns with the greatest potential to drive conversions and revenue growth from business or brand initiatives should be prioritized ahead of long-tail and low-volume search queries.

Diagnosis

Diagnosing SEO opportunities is similar to two patients coming to a doctor with exactly the same symptoms. A good physician will conduct a thorough examination before making a diagnosis and recommending a specific course of treatment. Even without an advanced degree in SEO, marketers have a wide variety of diagnostic tools (both free and proprietary) to determine what factors are keeping specific pages from ranking well within each keyword campaign.

Often, the site architecture prevents the search engine spiders from "crawling" certain sections of the site. Use of flash animation or Ajax prevents the spiders from reading your on-page content. A thorough SEO diagnosis should include an exhaustive analysis of the site architecture, code-level components, internal/external links, and on-page content.

Measured Execution

The results of your SEO diagnostics and opportunity analyses should drive your **iDirect** execution plan. Use the opportunity analysis to prioritize keywords and keyword markets with the greatest potential to drive increased conversions or revenue. Use the diagnostic report to identify specific pages on your site that require attention. Some keyword campaigns will require the development of new pages, or revisions to content on existing pages. In other cases, a well-orchestrated link-building campaign will increase the page rank of targeted pages.

Other times, strategically placing your keywords in the URL, title tags, headers, and on the page will improve search positioning on these targeted terms. Whatever the remediation plan, ensure that it can easily be adjusted based on new strategic priorities, changes in the competitive landscape, your time constraints, and internal resource availability.

Reporting and Analytics

With any ongoing SEO effort, success depends on maintaining full visibility into every tactic and outcome. Web analytics software provides both high-level summary reports of increases in traffic and conversions, as well as the detailed data that feed those reports. Custom reports enable you to evaluate the effectiveness of specific keyword campaigns or individual keywords. Depending on your level of data integration, marketers should strive to measure campaign effectiveness based on organic conversions, revenue, or net margin, rather than on traffic to the site.

A number of online tools enable you to track your keyword position compared to that of your competitors and estimate the volume of searches for your top keywords. These include Google Analytics to quantify your own site's organic traffic and top keywords and third-party tools such as Compete, SEMRush, and SpyFu to estimate your competitors' performance. Measuring your "share of search" in your most important keyword markets enables more accurate decision making and quicker responses to competitive threats.

This brief example demonstrates how strategic planning and sound data analytics can facilitate dramatic improvements in organic search results:

SEO CASE STUDY: CINEMA SITE

Background

One of the leading online destinations for checking movie show times and making advance movie ticket sales was in need of some major help with SEO. The site was historically driving the majority of its traffic through offline media, PR-driven brand awareness, and a costly paid search campaign. The rising cost of SEM and the hypercompetitive nature of the "movie ticket" vertical put pressure on the site to drive qualified traffic with nonbranded keywords via organic search.

Challenge

At the time of calling in outside expertise, 99 percent of the Web site was invisible to the search engines because of poor site architecture, lack of unique content/meta data, and limited links from authoritative sources.

Solution

A number of relatively simple changes to the site architecture resulted in dramatic improvements in site performance. We created new hierarchical site maps to allow the search engine spiders to fully crawl the site. In addition, all the URLs were redesigned to be "SEO friendly."

Essentially, this means eliminating extraneous parameters and putting the most important keywords toward the front of the URL string. So if the marketer wanted a particular page to rank highly for the query "Brad Pitt," the optimized URL would be www.domain.com/bradpitt. These changes led to immediate and dramatic increases in the number of pages indexed, organic traffic, and conversions.

With a solid architecture in place, **iDirect Marketing** expertise could build out new pages to increase traffic on a broader array of nonbranded keywords. These included authoritative pages on top actors, directors, and feature films. For any online business, these nonbranded, informational pages help build topic authority and can significantly increase traffic on long-tail and short-duration keywords.

Links from authoritative sites can increase your page rank and improve your position in the search results. The site generated a number of inbound links by developing viral links with fan networks and initiating some innovative link-building campaigns with movie distributors and theaters. This site was effective by providing the movie theaters with timely content about the latest releases. Much of this content was also picked up by bloggers and entertainment portals. Marketers in any industry can increase their inbound links by creating unique and relevant content and by making it easy to share among customers, partners, and other industry observers.

Results

Within a month of implementing these changes, the site went from having 150 pages indexed to over 146,000 pages indexed. Within days of changing the homepage title tag, the site moved from position number four to position number one in Google for its most critical keyword—"movie tickets."

As for the most important measurement, the site was able to increase organic traffic by 148 percent and increase tickets sold from organic search by 61 percent within one year.

THE "SECRET" OF SEM AND SEO SUCCESS

There are no secrets in SEM and SEO. The tools and techniques outlined here and elsewhere are well documented and generally available. What separates an adequate SEO/SEM effort from an exceptional one is constant referral to actionable data analytics and a commitment to ongoing testing and measurement. As with many of the other **iDirect** and **iBranding** resources described throughout this book, our direct marketing roots in being a data-driven discipline are paramount as we take advantage of digital interactions online.

The power to generate amazing results of both SEM and SEO lies in the continuous flow of data on every aspect of what is happening. It is yours in real time and on an ongoing basis; marketers can connect the dollars spent on a paid search campaign to the revenue earned through an online (or offline) conversion.

Marketers can know the number of searches for any given keyword; the number of times a visitor clicked on an organic search listing; and the activity, conversion, or revenue generated from each visit.

Cashing in on this end-to-end performance analysis requires a commitment to data integration and reporting before making an investment of time and dollars in search marketing. There is a lot of work to do upfront, but a commitment to rigorous data analysis affords unparalleled visibility into marketing effectiveness when you get started. The good news is that incremental investments made on a solidly built platform can produce astonishing ROI.

SHORT LIST OF BEST PRACTICES

- Always start with the data.
- Integrate your campaign data with backend conversion tracking.
- Establish your key performance indicators (KPIs) up front.
- Organize your data tracking and measurement before investing time and resources.
- Separate both your SEO and SEM campaigns into narrowly defined ad groups
- Employ data-driven prioritization going forward.
- Optimize SEM bids based on actual value rather than on clicks or conversions.

- Test, measure, test, measure, test, measure, test measure, onward and upward.

Keep in mind that SEM and SEO are the most targeted, most relevant, lowest-cost, and at the same time least intrusive advertising tools ever conceived. In the right hands they can realize the full potential of **iDirect Marketing**'s accountability, addressability, accessibility, and affordability.

Note

1. Quality score is a dynamic metric used by Google to determine the relevance of a paid search advertisement.

Chapter

7

Mobile: Holding iDirect in the Palm of Your Customer's Hand

Michael Becker

Cofounder and Vice President Mobile Strategies
of iLoop Mobile; Coauthor, *Web Marketing All-in-One
for Dummies*, Contributing Author to *Mobile
Internet for Dummies*, and Coeditor of the
International Journal of Mobile Marketing

We live in a mobile world. We live in a world where the majority of the global population carries with it a mobile phone or wirelessly enabled mobile terminal. This was not always the case. Motorola introduced the mobile phone in the early 1980s. In those days there were a few thousand mobile subscribers.

Analysts predicted that mobile phone use would grow in the years ahead. Fast-forward a quarter century, and mobile phone use has grown at a pace faster than anyone could have imagined. It will also become a driving force of the new **iDirect Marketing** and **iBranding** faster than anyone now imagines.

It is estimated that nearly 60 percent of the global population, around 4 billion people, now have a mobile phone.[1] In the United States mobile phone penetration has reached roughly 75 percent of the population, or 232 million individual mobile subscribers.[2] No other media channel, including television, radio, print, or even the Internet, reached this level of market penetration as quickly as did the mobile phone.[3]

The mobile phone's impact on society is significant. It is increasingly evident that the mobile phone changes consumer behavior, communication, content consumption, and commerce patterns. For instance, a recent study from the Mobile Marketing Association (www.mmaglobal.com) shows that a majority of survey respondents reports the mobile phone to be an integral part of their daily lives.[4] In fact, nearly 20 percent of the U.S. population has shut off its landline phone all together, preferring to have its mobile phone as its only phone. And an additional 14.5 percent of the population says that it has a landline but does not use it since the mobile phone is its primary telephone.[5]

This increased dependence on the mobile phone is affecting how we communicate. It is destined to become one of the most powerful channels for low-cost, highly effective **iDirect** performance. Nielsen Mobile, a leading mobile research firm, recently reported that voice is no longer the primary mobile phone communication channel used by mobile subscribers. This honor now falls to text messaging. Nielsen Mobile reports that the average mobile subscriber sends 357 text messages versus using 204 voice minutes.[6] Moreover, in addition to text messaging being used by nearly 58 percent of all mobile subscribers in the United States (Nielsen Mobile 2009) an increasing number of people (approximately 20 percent of mobile phone subscribers) now access the mobile Internet on their phones.[7]

Mobile Internet adoption shows no sign of slowing down; in fact it is picking up. For instance, mobile Internet use by Apple iPhone owners far exceeds that of other mobile phones. About 85 percent of iPhone users report using the mobile Internet (Nielsen Mobile 2009). More and more people are turning to their mobile phone for news and information, like real-time weather reports or even to buy pizza. Papa John's reported last year that it sold over $1 million worth of pizza in the first five months following the launch of its mobile Internet site, http://mobile.papajohns.com.[8]

There is no question about the incredible extent of the impact of mobile phones on society. They also are shaking up the practice of marketing. The mobile phone and its supporting collection of networks and service providers can be used by marketers and customers alike to communicate, deliver, and exchange value in an intimate, immediate, and cost-effective manner. What is not clear for many marketers is exactly how this new channel works and how it can be effectively employed to deliver reciprocal value between the marketer and the mobile phone user.

This chapter reviews the choices marketers must consider to effectively use this highly personal, interactive, new star performer in the **iDirect** media spectrum. We begin by defining the mobile channel and the numerous modes of engagement that are supported through it. We then discuss the factors marketers must examine when incorporating mobile marketing into their corporate and marketing strategies. Finally, the chapter concludes with a summary of resources you can consult to further your use of mobile marketing and its transformational effect on **iDirect Marketing** and **iBranding** practices.

UNVEILING THE MOBILE CHANNEL

Compared to the analog, voice-dedicated 30-ounce "bricks" that were once carried by road warriors and early adopters, the majority of today's mobile phones would be difficult to recognize. On the one hand the mobile phone of today can be a lightweight dedicated device for making and receiving phone calls or for performing rudimentary data service, such as accessing the Internet or sending text messages. On the other hand the mobile phone can be a full-featured, multipurpose, high-bandwidth, networked, multimodal, interactive information, communication, and commerce tool. The former is commonly referred to as a traditional, or featured, mobile phone, and the latter is referred to as a smartphone.

There is a third class of mobile device emerging—the dedicated mobile terminal, such as the Apple iPod touch, Sony PSP, netbook, and Amazon Kindle—which also needs to be kept in mind by the marketer. Each of these devices has some form of wireless connectivity, either WiFi or an embedded wireless broadband access card as in the case of the Kindle, that can support interactive marketing. Currently the majority of mobile subscribers, roughly 87 percent, carries a traditional mobile phone as its primary phone. The other subscribers are the early adopters of smartphones.[9] Dedicated devices are not considered in mobile usage adoption numbers since they are considered a "secondary" device used by mobile subscribers or considered in another class entirely. The full-featured, data-rich, smartphone category includes the Apple iPhone, Google Android, Palm, BlackBerry, Microsoft Windows, and Nokia Symbian. The market share for this category is multiplying at a phenomenal rate.

Many consider the mobile channel as one big generic pipe, but this view is a misinformed generalization. Actually, there are numerous interactive communication, delivery, and exchange paths that are used to navigate the mobile channel and interact

Figure 7.1   The paths through the mobile channel.
Courtesy of iLoop Mobile Inc.

with one's audience. These paths include voice, text messaging, multimedia messaging, e-mail, Internet, mobile Internet, Bluetooth, and applications.[10] (See Figure 7.1.)

The following is a brief definition of each path:

- *SMS* refers to short message service. This is also commonly known as text messaging, and is composed of an alphanumeric message consisting of 160 characters or less delivered through the mobile channel.
- *MMS* refers to multimedia messaging service. This specifically refers to a unique protocol for exchanging digital content, such as videos, pictures, and audio content via the mobile channel. The abbreviation MMS is often generically used for all forms of digital content, even if the delivery does not follow the proper MMS protocol.
- *E-mail* refers to the delivery of e-mail content through the mobile channel.

- *Voice* refers to the voice channel of the phone and, for the purposes of mobile marketing, can take the form of talking with a live person such as an individual at a call center, who in turn may trigger mobile data services as a response to the call, or through an interactive voice response (IVR) system.

- *Internet* refers to the ability of the mobile device to connect to the Internet for a wide range of data-enabled services, including the mobile Web, applications, content services like streaming video (e.g., mobile TV) as well as mobile carrier managed portals, such as Verizon V Cast or T-Mobile T-zones.

- *Mobile Web* refers to the experience of browsing the Internet via the mobile phone.

- *Bluetooth* refers to the short-range Bluetooth radio channel, typically used to connect a phone with wireless headsets and related periphery devices, but it can also be used to deliver content to the mobile phone.

- *Applications* refer to software utilities and services downloaded to the mobile phone.

DEFINING MOBILE MARKETING

Here is a simplified approach to mobile marketing. First take the marketing part, as defined by the American Marketing Association (http://www.marketingpower.com/): "The activity, set of institutions, and processes for creating, communicating, delivering, and exchanging offerings that have value for customers, clients, partners, and society at large."[11] Then mobile marketing can be viewed as the set of activities, institutions, and processes employed by marketers to communicate, deliver, and exchange value with members of their audience through and with the mobile channel.[12]

Mobile marketing is performed in two ways, either directly or indirectly. Mobile direct marketing refers to the practice of marketing directly to individuals via the mobile channel. Mobile direct marketing can be either proactive "push" marketing or passive "pull" marketing. With the proactive form a marketer proactively initiates an engagement with an individual; for example, a marketer may send a text message directly to an individual's phone. With the passive form the marketer can setup a mobile Web site or voice response channel and a consumer initiates the interaction by visiting the site or calling into the voice service. This moves the mobile phone into being a prominent next-generation **iDirect Marketing** component.

MARKETER BEWARE

In order to practice proactive, push mobile marketing, marketers must receive prior consent. The opt-in from the individual before initiating any form of direct communication through the mobile channel is a vital part of the process. The requirement for prior consent is dictated by both industry best practices and government regulation such as the guidelines published by the Mobile Marketing Association (www.mmaglobal.com) and Direct Marketing Association (www.the-dma.org).

Marketers should heed the fact that a single consumer response to a call-to-action (i.e., an ad hoc response), does not denote permission for ongoing interaction. The marketer must get explicit permission for ongoing interaction. In order to connect with an individual or to obtain permission for ongoing interaction, the marketer can utilize alternative channels and make an offer with a call to action. The use of alterative means to invite someone to engage in mobile marketing by phone or texting is a common **iDirect** practice.

Mobile can be used in combination with both traditional and new media channels such as television, radio, outdoor media, print media, Internet, and e-mail. This practice is referred to as *indirect mobile marketing*. For example, on May 14, 2009, during a television airing of *American Idol* viewers were invited to text "alive" to the common short code 90999 to donate $5 to Keep a Child Alive (www.keepachildalive.com), an organization dedicated to helping fight the spread of HIV/AIDS. The group reportedly received over $450,000 from 90,000 donors from this one night.[13] In another example Money Mailer (www.moneymailer.com), a leading provider of direct marketing services, reports tremendous uplift on coupon redemption and high return on investment (ROI) for marketing programs, often exceeding a 12 percent redemption rate with mobile-enhanced shared mail coupons.[14] (See Figure 7.2.)

INTERFACING MOBILE MARKETING WITH YOUR OVERALL STRATEGY

Based on the previously offered definition of mobile marketing, how do marketers bring mobile marketing into their overall cor-

Figure 7.2 Money Mailer shared mail coupon with mobile enhancement.
Courtesy of Money Mailer LLC

porate and marketing strategies? The purpose of a marketing strategy is to marshal, align, and budget the necessary organizational and industry resources to achieve an organization's overall aims. In other words, strategy and tactics are the bridge that connects organizational aspirations on the one hand and the concrete actions needed to fulfill the plan on the other hand.

In order to develop a sound mobile marketing strategy, it is imperative that you first take a broad view of your business. You need to look at the factors that affect your overall strategy before deciding on where mobile marketing fits to greatest advantage. Mobile marketing is not an end unto itself, but rather an extraordinarily versatile new tool put at your command by extraordinary advances in technology. It is one of many capabilities within your **iDirect** and **iBranding** arsenal to help you achieve your marketing goals. First and foremost, you need:

- A very clear picture of the target audience you want to reach, ideally segmented into individual constituencies. You want as detailed a profile as possible of each constituent segment or each individual constituent.
- An understanding and clear articulation of the value your product or service delivers to the market and how it meets the needs of each constituent in the audience.
- A clear articulation of company goals in an easily understandable and measurable fashion.

Effective mobile marketing is dependant on seven influential factors that drive the applicability of strategic decision making.[15]

Table 7.1 summarizes these factors. Careful consideration of each of the operational factors must be consciously managed by the marketer for best mobile marketing results.

To summarize the above factors, here is a mobile path mass-market applicability scorecard (Table 7.2).

Table 7.1 Mobile Marketing Applicability Factors

Factor	Description	Impact example
Interoperability	Refers to whether or not a particular mobile path or capability, such as SMS or camera functions, work across mobile operator and wireless networks and also if the capability is supported on available mobile devices.	SMS is supported on nearly 99 percent of all phones and is interoperable across almost all major mobile operator networks. Mobile marketing via applicable Bluetooth is supported on a limited number of mobile handsets and networks. To this end SMS has mass-market reach, while Bluetooth does not.
Standards and policies	Refers to whether or not there are both business and technical standards and industry policies to govern the effective use of a particular mobile path or capability.	The Mobile Marketing Association (www.mmaglobal.com) has established clear and concise industry guidelines, "MMA Consumer Best Practices." These guidelines apply to many forms of mass-market mobile marketing paths; such as SMS, mobile Web, and voice, but is limited in relation to niche market paths, such as applications. To this end, SMS, voice, and mobile Web have clear standards, while standards and laws for the other channels are still emerging.
Mobile device adoption	Considers the extent to which a particular mobile device model, capability, and service has proliferated in the market and is in the hands of mobile subscribers.	The Motorola Razr and similar traditional phones have significant market penetration and are ideal for voice and SMS and limited mobile Internet use. Smartphones account for approximately 12 percent

of overall mobile phone market share. The iPhone accounts for less than 2 percent. Both are perfect for downloadable applications and related services. To this end, marketers should understand the types of phones people are using. If they promote a service, for example, an iPhone application, they should understand that their market reach today will be limited to less than 2 percent of the mass market.

Mobile device feature adoption   Considers the extent to which a particular mobile device capability and feature has been adopted by mobile subscribers.

An estimated 58 percent of mobile subscribers use text messaging, while 27 percent regularly access the mobile Internet, and only 2 percent download applications. To this end, if a marketer is looking to launch a mobile marketing program, it is important to consider what people do with their phones.

Mobile path health   Considers the extent to which the mobile channel and a particular path is free from industry value system friction.

Voice is an extremely open and well-understood channel, as is the mobile Internet. While SMS is technically mature, there is still significant channel friction resulting from the necessity of mobile operator approval and ongoing compliance monitoring and adherence requirements. With MMS the process is almost completely blocked because of

(continued on next page)

Table 7.1 (continued)

Factor	Description	Impact example
		industry friction. A marketer should understand the health of a mobile path so that industry friction does not affect a program or the organization's strategy in using the channel.
Geography	Considers the extent to which geography plays a role in the launching of mobile programs.	Industry rules, laws, and regulations; mobile devices; carrier networks; and execution policies vary significantly among regions and within individual countries around the world. For example, common short codes, the five- to six-digit codes used for commercially addressing text messaging (see www.usshortcodes.com), do not work across country borders.
Consumer profiles	Recognizes the fact that consumer profile factors, including age, gender, ethnicity, education, income, device type used, network, behavior, physiographic profile, and preferences all affect a marketer's audience members' potential for engagement and how effective a particular mobile marketing strategy or tactic may be.	In the United States it is well understood that text messaging adoption averages approximately 58 percent for the overall population; however, its use varies greatly, 25–84 percent; across various mobile subscriber profile factors (Nielsen Mobile 2009). Similarly phone model usage, such as the iPhone, also varies by profiles.

Table 7.2 Mobile Path Mass-Marketing Applicability Scorecard

Factor	Voice	SMS	Mobile Internet	MMS	E-mail	Bluetooth	Internet	Internet/application
Inter-operability	X	X	X	X			X	
Standards and policies	X	X	X		X		X	
Mobile device adoption	X	X	X	X				
Mobile device feature adoption	X	X		X				
Mobile channel health	X	X	X					
Geography	X		X				X	
Consumer profile	X	X	X					
Applicability rate	7/7	6/7	6/7	3/7	1/7	0/7	3/7	0/7

As you can see from the scorecard, voice, SMS, and the mobile Internet work well for mass-market programs and consumer engagement, while the other paths are not and should be considered for niche markets. Figure 7.3 illustrates this point.

HOW MARKETERS MAKE MOBILE PAY OFF

There are as many things you can do with mobile marketing as there are creative ideas that marketers can come up with. We have found that one of the best ways to classify mobile marketing programs is through the lens of the customer life cycle.

Marketers should consider whether or not their program is for the purposes of acquiring new customers; developing, retaining, or expanding existing relationships; or supporting and/or encour-

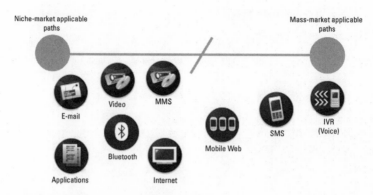

Figure 7.3 Mobile path marketing mapping.
Courtesy of iLoop Mobile

aging customs to virally share their experiences with the brand engagement. Table 7.3 highlights seven solid examples of mobile marketing in action.

THE IMPORTANCE OF GETTING EXECUTION RIGHT

The final step in developing a mobile marketing strategy is the focus on execution. There are five building blocks (see Table 7.4) to consider when it comes to executing your mobile marketing creative ideas—strategy, creative, tactical execution, platform (technology), and analytics and measurement that must be considered.[16]

Figure 7.4 shows the relationship between each of these building blocks and helps illustrate the mobile marketing expertise continuum.

Two ways to look at the know-how needed for success with **iDirect** influenced mobile marketing are represented in Figure 7.4 by the expertise triangles superimposed on the five blocks. There are two expertise triangles, one for marketing expertise and the other for technology and solutions expertise. Mobile marketing requires a significant amount of both. Very few companies succeeded in the long term without mastering each of these aspects

Table 7.3 Featured Mobile Marketing Case Studies

Campaign	Life cycle stage(s)	Description
Obama for America[1]	Customer acquisition; relationship; support; word-of-mouth	Mobile marketing played a key role in President Obama's race for the White House. The Obama for America team used text alerts, a mobile Web site, mobile content delivery, interactive voice, iPhone applications, and more to help win the election. Members of Obama's team announced the vice president nomination via text messaging, recruited volunteers via text, collected first-hand voter input and questions via voice, shared content, stimulated voters to engage their friends, and so much more through all the mobile channels. They promoted his programs directly though the mobile channel, as well as through the mobile enhancement of traditional and new media, including flyers, social networking Web sites, bumper stickers, the Internet, and more. This campaign clearly demonstrates that mobile marketing is effective within a multiyear, multichannel strategy looking to drive both national as well as regional engagement.
Daisy Maids[2]	Customer acquisition	In early 2009 a regional Salt Lake City Daisy Maids franchise sponsored a contest that was promoted via the radio. The sponsorship cost $1,000 and consisted of an ad being placed at the end of each text response sent to each listener that opted into the contest. The call to action in the radio spot had people texting in to enter to win four pairs of tickets to a concert. The spot ran for one week, and 24,000 people responded via text to opt-in for the contest with each receiving a confirmation message via text, within the response was the franchise ad which

(continued on next page)

109

Table 7.3 (continued)

Campaign	Life cycle stage(s)	Description
		was inserted at the end of the response: "Need a clean house, reply CLEAN." In total, 700 replied "CLEAN" and 80 percent, or 560, of these respondents became new customers. This case emphasizes the point that huge response rates are not needed to have a significant bottom-line impact on the marketer's business.
Keep a Child Alive[3]	Donor acquisition; relationship-building	On May 14, 2009, during a television airing of *American Idol* viewers were invited to text "Alive" to the common short code 90999 to donate $5 to Keep a Child Alive (www.keepachildalive.com), an organization dedicated to helping fight the spread of HIV/AIDS. The group reportedly received over $450,000 from 90,000 donors from this one night's showing. Cause and philanthropic endeavors are a key component of many marketing strategies. To date the Mobile Giving Foundation (http://www.mobilegiving.org/Charities.aspx) and its application partners help over 100 charities raise money for their causes. Calls to action for giving are promoted via the Web, mobile Internet, print, at live events, on television and radio, and via other channels. Mobile Giving Foundation partners include iLoop Mobile, mGive, distributive networks, and others.
TCBY and Money Mailer Couponing[4]		A TCBY frozen yogurt franchise began working with the direct marketing company Money Mailer in the early part of 2009. The franchise promoted a mobile call to action, "FREE YOGURT text KEYWORD to SHORT CODE" on table tops, banners, window clings, reader boards, the product cups, and related media in order to generate opt-ins and drive traffic to the store. In a short period

of time the campaign generated 500 opt-ins and a 12 percent redemption rate. Staff members were trained to present the label facing the customer, they suggested the new program to the customer, and they explained how to opt-in and that it is free to them. The store phone number was placed in the welcome text message so customers would know which TCBY location to go to. Yes, even small businesses can succeed with mobile marketing and turn once inert one-way marketing campaigns into **iDirect** channels.

| Jaguar[5] | Customer acquisition | In 2008 Jaguar ran a two-month mobile advertising campaign in the United States promoting the release of the new 2009 Jaguar XF, a high-end luxury car. According to Mischler, 15 million ad impressions drove over 85,000 unique visitors to the campaign's mobile Web site. These visitors downloaded 12,000 videos and 16,000 wallpapers. In addition, 1.6 percent of the visitors requested brochures, and 2.6 percent requested test drives at a dealer near them. Similar campaign results can be seen throughout the auto industry. There is no doubt that mobile plays a key role engaging consumers and driving customers and sales to retail in a cost-effective manner. |
| Direct Marketing Association DMA 08[6] | Customer care | During its 2008 annual event, DMA 08, the Direct Marketing Association (www.the-dma.org) offered a number of mobile services, including a mobile concierge service, text alert services, and mobile Web site. For example, the mobile concierge service allowed attendees of the event to text a question, any questions, to a short code during the event, and a concierge monitoring the information booth at the show would respond in real time with an answer to the |

(continued on next page)

Table 7.3 (continued)

Campaign	Life cycle stage(s)	Description
		question. In addition, attendees could visit the show's mobile Web site for the event schedule and other show information. The CTIA (www.ctia.org) runs similar services at its events, including a booth finder, vote and polling services, and a wide range of other customer engagement/care services.
Transformers mobile campaign[7]	Viral and word of mouth	For some time movie and entertainment studios have been embracing mobile marketing. E! Online for example offers iPhone apps, text alerts, games, mobile Internet sites (e.g., http://eonline.mobi/), see http://www.eonline.com/everywhere/mobile/index.jsp. They're also using voice and interactive voice services. For example, Paramount Pictures with the 2009 release of *Transformers* had a mobile campaign where a user could use an online application to have the film's Optimus Prime character call his or her friend with a custom message along with a call to action to both create their own message and buy the *Transformers* DVD. It has been reported that the campaign drove more than 1.27 million unique recipients in 20 days to engage with the mobile medium.

1. Khan, M. A., "Why Barack Obama Is Mobile Marketer of the Year," 2009, retrieved May 31, 2009, http://www.mobilemarketer.com/cms/news/advertising/2462.html.2009.

2. Willmore, C., "HipCricket Christine Willmore 80% Close Rate for Daisy Maids," 2009, retrieved May 31, 2009, http://www.youtube.com/watch?v=-CCcsHgCSE4.

3. Keep a Child Alive, "Keep a Child Alive Raised $450,000 during *American Idol*," May 14, 2009, retrieved May 23, 2009, http://mobilegivinginsider.com/post/10788376/keep-a-child-alive-raised-450-000-during-american.

4. Gray, S., and M. Becker, "Mobile Couponing: Generating Sales and Consumer Engagement," presented at the Mobile Labs Webinar series, San Jose, CA, June 23, 2009.

5. Mischler, A., and M Becker, "Mobile Web Marketing: Usage and Attitudes … and the 10 Mistakes," paper presented at the Direct Marketing Association, 2008.

6. DMA 08, www.the-dma.org.

7. Andronikov, A. S., "Mobile as an Effective Media Channel for Movie Studios, 2009, retrieved May 31, 2009, http://www.mobilemarketer.com/cms/opinion/columns/3168.html

Table 7.4 Strategic and Tactical Building Blocks of Mobile Marketing

Building block	Description
Strategy	As discussed, strategy is how the company marshals and aligns the necessary organizational and industry resources in order to achieve its overall aims. To this end all the pertinent factors must be considered.
Creative	The creative block addresses all the elements marketers need to pull together and develop to create the look, feel, and flow of their mobile marketing program(s). This includes content, images, color schemes, user experience, user flows, and so on. It covers any messaging rhetoric, or communication plan, marketers use in their content and calls to action, and all the campaign elements that will set them apart from the competitive pack. Marketers' creative should give their program a uniqueness that reflects the intent of the program (remember—content selections will be key to creating uniqueness). Marketers should not let preconceived notions of what they think can and can't be done limit their creativity. Rather, they should consider consulting with a mobile marketing expert—that is if they feel blocked—to help them develop a program within their available budget and within the capabilities of their available resources. Mobile marketing need not be complicated or expensive to have an impact.
Tactical execution	Tactical execution addresses all the detailed steps and minutia of a marketer's mobile marketing initiatives from conception, to delivery, through maintenance, and eventually to shut down. (See the following section for an additional discussion of tactical execution.)
Platform (technology)	Platform (technology) is the next block in the mobile marketing matrix, and it addresses all the technology and related management know-how (software, hardware, applications, connections with mobile carriers, etc.) needed for launching marketing programs in one or more of the mobile channel paths.

(continued on next page)

Table 7.4 (continued)

Building block	Description
Analytics and measurement	The analytics and measurement block is tightly tied to the platform (technology) block in that the data for the analytics and measurement are collected by the mobile marketing platform/solution. Analytics and measurement, however, are a construct that addresses not only the collection of the data, but also the analysis of the data and the generation of useful knowledge from them. The data analytics lead to action-oriented decision making that further affects future strategic, creative, tactical execution, and platform decisions. Moreover, marketers may obtain tremendous insight into their audience's behaviors and preferences when combining mobile marketing data with traditional and new media marketing program results.

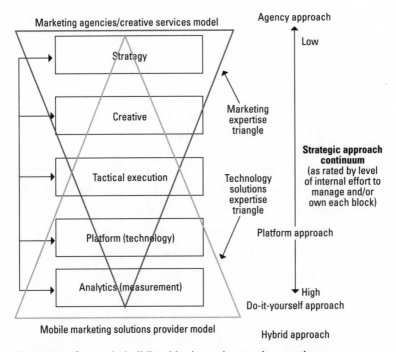

Figure 7.4 Strategic building blocks and expertise continuum.

of mobile marketing. Most companies perform well at only one end of the spectrum or the other. They either focus on developing a deep level of technology expertise, or they develop brilliant marketing strategy and creative expertise. More often than not marketers start by hiring an agency to launch a handful of initiatives; that is, they'll outsource the effort to launch programs. Over time, as they get comfortable with the medium, they'll begin to take more control of the process in-house. Often they wind up adopting a platform approach, in which they license a mobile marketing solutions platform, or hybrid approach, where they'll control parts of each block and partner for other parts.

For marketers to complete the resourcing and planning of their mobile marketing strategy, it is necessary to understand upfront investments and ignore tactical campaign expenses. There is also the requirement of developing a campaign time line. For insight into these considerations, review the article "Mobile Marketing Budgeting: A Look at Mobile Marketing Cost Centers and Timeline" at http://iloopmobile.com/blog/?p=216.

TACTICAL CONSIDERATIONS FOR iDIRECT MOBILE CAMPAIGNS

Once you have a clear understanding of the factors that affect utilizing mobile marketing to reach your target audience and have a clear view of strategic direction, you can begin to tap the almost limitless number of interactions that are possible.

Mobile marketing has been used to successfully engage consumers at every stage of the customer life cycle. Marketers can use mobile marketing to:

- Acquire new customers.
- Increase and reward customer loyalty.
- Generate brand awareness.
- Monetize content.
- Provide convenient, interactive customer service.
- Drive attendance to live events and retail.
- Promote products and services, often through couponing, sweepstakes, and other promotions.
- Create viral customer-to-customer brand reinforcement.
- Facilitate cause-related marketing.

Often, the goal for these programs is to build and maintain an opt-in database of mobile phone numbers the owners of which have expressed interest in the proposition and given permission to receive future communication from the marketer. This data mart of phone numbers may in fact become the **iDirect** marketer's most important asset. It is common knowledge that the mobile phone number changes less often than people's e-mail, home, and

Table 7.5 Staying Current on Mobile Marketing

Source	Description
Publications	Numerous books and publications For a short list of important publications see M. Becker, "Mobile Marketing Statistics and Resources" at http://iloopmobile.com/blog/wp-admin/page.php?=editpost=59.
Blogs	There are numerous leading industry blogs, including: http://www.mobithinking.com http://www.mobilemarketingwatch.com http://www.smstextnews.com http:www.Moconews.net http://www.fiercewireless.com/ http://www.wikipedia.com http://www.mobilecrunch.com http://www.mobileactive.org http://www.mobilemarketingmagazine.co.uk http://blog.nielsen.com/nielsenwire/tag/mobile-internet/
Commercial research	There are a number of very reliable commercial research groups reporting on mobile marketing effectiveness: comScore, Nielsen Mobile, Yankee Group, Frost & Sullivan, The Garnter Group, The Aberdeen Group, and countless others all can be accessed on the Internet.
Industry service providers and social networking sites	Many service providers offer access to incredibly insightful market data from their company Web sites and their social networking presence on Facebook, Twitter, and YouTube. These players include, but are not limited to Bango, iLoop Mobile, Millennial Media, Ad Mob, dotMobi, and U.S. Short Codes Administration.

(continued on next page)

Table 7.5 (continued)

Source	Description
Industry trade groups	The leading mobile marketing industry trade groups are the Mobile Marketing Association, the Direct Marketing Association, The Direct Marketing Education Foundation, the Internet Advertising Bureau, InMobile.org, dotMobi Advisory Group, CTIA, 3GSM, and others.

work phone numbers and home or work addresses. In fact, the mobile phone number often becomes a global identification number. For marketers it represents what may be the most reliable form of interactive engagement. Mobile Marketer (www.mobilemarketer.com) is a fantastic resource for viewing examples of mobile marketing programs from industry-leading brands and entrepreneurial start-ups.

The most frequently used campaign tactics for achieving your mobile marketing objectives include:

- Mobile advertising with the insertion of:
  - Interactive banner and text ads within mobile Web sites.
  - Interactive banner and text ads on mobile carrier portals.
  - Mobile search.
  - Sponsored third-party news and information text alerts.
  - In-stream ads during video or audio programming.
- Inclusion of text messaging calls to action and mobile Internet links, second and third bar codes on product packages, in print ads or on TV, such as "Text Win to 12345" (i.e., mobile enhancement of traditional media).
- Text messaging sweepstakes, voting, contests, ad hoc promotions. and/or list building.
- Coupons or promotions via SMS.
- Applications, with the most popular being the multitude available for iPhone.
- Direct marketing promotion and sales to permission-based lists.

NOW IT'S YOUR TURN

Mobile marketing is an emerging practice. Early evidence shows that it can be an extremely effective means of acquiring new customers, engaging with them and boosting your bottom line with a wide range of measurable activities. Unlike the Web where advancing technology, consumer adoption, and marketer employment of the new channel happened in parallel, mobile marketers mostly find themselves behind the consumer adoption curve. The technology is here, and consumers have bought into the medium in droves. In fact for many it is their primary means of communication. It is time for marketers to realize that there is a lot of catching up to do and to start fully embracing this channel in support of intimate, interactive, engaging relationships with the members of their target audience.

Your best connection to the world around you and the world far beyond you sits in the palm of your hand. It also happens to be where the new always-on, always-present **iDirect Marketing** and **iBranding** opportunities of the future reside. How well you put the cell phone to use in marketing directly can result in being first to gain a tremendous competitive advantage.

Notes

1. "Mobile Phone Subscribers Pass 4 Billion Mark," *Cellular-news*, December 13, 2008, retrieved May 23, 2009, http://www.cellular-news.com/story/35298.php.
2. "Iphone Hype Holds Up" *ComScore*, 2009, http://www.marketwire.com/press-release/MMetrics-833439.html.
3. Ahonen, T., "Putting 2.7 Billion in Context: Mobile Phone Users," retrieved May 23, 2009, http://communities-dominate.blogs.com/brands/2007/01/putting_27_bill.html.
4. Mobile Marketing Association, Mobile Attitude & Usage Study, 2008.
5. Blumberg, S. J., and J. V. Luke, Wireless Substitution: Early Release of Estimates from the National Health Interview Survey, July–December 2008, retrieved May 23, 2009, http://www.cdc.gov/nchs/data/nhis/earlyrelease/wireless200905.htm.
6. Reardon, M, "Americans Text More than They Talk," retrieved May 23, 2009, http://news.cnet.com/8301-1035_3-10048257-94.html.2008.
7. McLaren, J., "The Next Big Things: Mobile Internet & Applications—Gaining Momentum," *comScore*, 2009, (conference proceeding).
8. Khan, M. A., "Papa John's Generates $1M in Mobile Web Sales," 2009, retrieved May 23, 2009, http://www.mobilemarketer.com/cms/authors/5.html.
9. McLaren, J., "The Next Big Things: Mobile Internet & Applications—Gaining Momentum."
10. Arnold, J., I. Lurie, M. Dickinson, E. Marsten, and M. Becker, *Web Marketing All-in-One Desk Reference for Dummies* (Indianapolis: Wiley, 2009).
11. Lotti, M., and D. Lehmann, AMA Definition of Marketing, 2007, retrieved May 23, 2009, http://www.marketingpower.

com/Community/ARC/Pages/Additional/Definition/default. aspx.

12. Arnold et al., *Web Marketing All-in-One Desk Reference for Dummies*.

13. Keep a Child Alive Raised $450,000 during *American Idol*, May 14, 2009, retrieved May 23, 2009, from http://mobile givinginsider.com/post/107886376/keep-a-child-alive-raised-450-000-during-american.

14. Gray, S., and M. Becker, "Mobile Couponing: Generating Sales and Consumer Engagement," Webinar presented at the Mobile Labs Webinar series, San Jose, CA, 2009, http:// resourcecenter.iloopmobile.com/?q=node/183.

15. Becker, M., "What Is in the Data? Leveraging Mobile Ad Network Data," *Journal of Targeting, Measurement and Analysis for Marketing*, 16(1), 2007, pp. 3–6.

16. Becker, M., "Mobile Marketing's Strategic Building Blocks," 2008, retrieved May 23, 2009, http://iloopmobile.com/blog/ ?p=230.

Chapter
8

Using Psychology to Drive Digital Behavior

Melissa Read, Ph.D.

Vice President of Research and Innovation, Engauge

If marketing is about connecting with people to drive behavior, then marketing is about psychology. Yet in the marketing environment we seldom hear this word. Is it rightfully something outside a businessperson's concern? I certainly hope not. Psychology holds the key to everything we are and everything we do. It explains how we think, our perceptions of the world, and what drives our every action. And when it comes to making a purchase decision, it's right there guiding our choice.

For over 100 years, academics in psychology have carefully studied the human brain and the behavior it controls. Those who studied human judgment discovered how decisions are made and how to influence their outcomes. Those who studied human vision discovered how to change perception. Those who studied human behavior discovered how to drive action. Academics in psychology have spent over 100 years in their ivory towers, learning how to predict and *influence* what people do. But when it comes to marketing, their findings have largely been ignored.

The most comprehensive understanding of human behavior lives in dusty journal stacks on university library shelves. And when these journals are consulted, the greatest discoveries ever made about *why* people do what they do are written in a language that business doesn't understand. What a missed opportunity. So many powerful drivers of behavior are dormant, ever awaiting application. So why have psychology and business been separated? Truth is, the space between them is vast. Language divides them. Philosophies divide them. Longstanding habits divide them. With so much space between them, the experts in each discipline rarely talk to each other.

But they should, because with psychology we can discover things about our customers that they don't know about themselves. With the insight that only psychology provides, we have the power to change perceptions and to drive action. So it's high time to start building bridges between psychology and business. When we do, we will experience a degree of relevance in marketing that has yet to be seen.

IT'S ABOUT HAVING A NEW KIND OF CONVERSATION

In ancient times, the marketing channel was almost exclusively a person, and that person in many ways served as the brand. At the bazaar, marketing was largely a persuasive, one-to-one conversation. And often that was enough to drive action.

Over the last century, marketing channels began to evolve along with the evolution of technology. Radio and TV joined newspapers and magazines as primary communication channels. We experienced the growth of mass, one-way, brand-to-consumer communication. The days of one-to-one conversation with our customers were largely over. Marketing message distribution became a broadside, fired at everyone. In the morning, we'd listen to the radio and perhaps read a newspaper on our commute. We'd work the eight-hour day and then come home to watch several hours of prime-time TV at night. There were a limited number of mass communication channels, and our involvement with those channels was patterned and predictable. There was little opportunity for a direct response. So we just listened.

But those were simpler times. Today, new media channels emerge in rapid succession and present us with far more options than ever before. With the advent of these channels, the media consumption pattern has fully transformed into a two-way experience. We have returned to the conversation we once had with brands in ancient civilizations. But today's conversation is different from anything that came before. It is both *more* and *less* personal. New media channels allow for two-way dialogue as in ancient times, but on a profoundly accessible and scalable basis. This has brought both new complexity and new simplicity to our lives.

Just look at the world that emerging media have created in the past decade. It allows asynchronous communication with people in other time zones whom we've never met. It allows us to share, store, and acquire knowledge at a fantastically rapid pace. It allows us to grow and foster social networks that are larger and longer lasting than our free time and memory ever permitted. We engage in new behaviors, like media snacking—consuming bite-sized pieces of media from various places daily. We engage in media multitasking—tuning in to more than one media channel and dividing our attention between them.

The interactive digital communication that drives **iDirect Marketing** is perhaps the greatest advance in marketing technology since the advent of Henry Ford's mass production assembly line and the mass marketing it inspired. This is not only because of what **iDirect** communication can do for us today, but because of everything we'll build on top of it in the future. In this new space, we see ourselves in new ways. We create new identities. We have greater expectations. We are no longer comfortable just listening. We believe that we should be able to respond directly to the biggest brands, and we believe that the biggest brands should respond directly to us.

The conversation businesses now can have with consumers has been transformed, and the rules of customer engagement have been transformed in turn. To engage our customers today, we can no longer connect *unidirectionally* across a single high-volume channel. Today, the customer-brand relationship is a summation of *multidirectional* connections from a multitude of communication channels. If we really want to engage our customers, we must find a way to step back and understand the psychology behind these interactions. We must find a way to make our conversation feel as personal as it did when we were selling one to one in the ancient village bazaar.

DRIVING PERCEPTION, INTERACTION, AND DECISION MAKING

With the emergence of digital media and the complexity that they bring, the need to apply psychological insights has never been greater. Psychology drives perception, interaction, decision making, and ultimately purchase choice.

So what role should psychology play in today's transformed marketing mix? How can psychology add value beyond what we already gain from tried-and-true marketing methods like analytics assessment, ethnographic observation, and creative inspiration?

Simply put, these proven methods tell us the *how* and the *what* in marketing, but often not the *why*. That is, they help inform *how* we connect with consumers and *what* we say, but don't always explain *why* we experience success or failure in connecting with customers and driving sales.

Here's an example of the "why factor." Let's say we want to determine the best background color for a fast-food banner campaign. We've narrowed it down to two choices, red or blue. Analytics assessment can tell us that the red banner produces significantly greater click-through rates when compared to the blue one. Ethnography can tell us that customers tend to like the red banner more than the blue one when viewing it in their homes. Creative can gain inspiration from fast-food menus and tell us to use the red color to be consistent with the color on the menu that drives the most sales. And as a result of all these inputs or even just one, we'd likely end up choosing the red banner over the blue one, and we'd likely end up getting decent results because of our choice.

But it's only an understanding of human psychology that can tell us *why* a red background is the better choice. Only psychology can tell us that the brain is hardwired to see blue as an appetite suppressant across environments and cultures. This is to the result of unpleasant evolutionarily reactions to eating blue mold and the infrequent occurrence of blue in natural food. Only psychology can tell us that reds and browns and yellows increase appetite because these colors frequently occur naturally in food and because these were the colors we needed to detect long ago when we searched for fruit among the trees. Psychology explains *why* our analytics assessment shows significantly more click-throughs for the red banner, *why* our customers tended to like the red banner more when viewing it in their homes, and *why* the red menu drives the most restaurant sales.

When we understand the psychological underpinnings of the results we produce by color choice, we can inform more than just our current marketing campaign, but future campaigns as well. And going beyond marketing communication, psychology can tell us what color to use in a restaurant, a grocery store, or our dining room. Understanding "why," specific colors drive specific results gives us the power to make the best choices before creative is produced. It makes us smarter as marketers, and it in turn protects our timelines and budgets.

Marketers will continue to get value from methods like analytics assessment, ethnography, and creative inspiration. Most of the time, using just one of these methods can point marketers in the right direction. And when these methods are used in combination, they can be a potent force. But even combined, these methods are not enough. Psychological insight is the missing piece that brings meaning to the rest—the piece that explains *why* we succeed or fail. One hundred years of sound scientific psychological findings await us as a blueprint for the new **iDirect** and **iBranding** era—if we only choose to leverage them.

PSYCHOLOGY AS A FORCE IN THE DIGITAL REVOLUTION

Psychology is at work in every successful interactive and direct marketing initiative. Brands like Facebook, Twitter, and LinkedIn are great examples. Each faces the challenge of becoming a viable direct marketing channel. Each has an audience that experiences deep engagement with the brand.

How do these brands elicit such deep engagement? Why do their audiences interact with them so frequently? Among the drivers is the psychology of human motivation. Human motivation is the science of instincts, drives, and needs. Motivation research suggests that people are driven by a hierarchy of needs. When lower-level needs are met, like hunger, thirst, and safety, people next are motivated by higher-level needs, such as belongingness.

The fundamental need for belongingness drives our desire to form friendships as well as romantic partnerships. It motivates our desire to share our lives with one another. Belongingness inspires us to know others and to be known by them. It not only explains why brands that facilitate social connection create deep customer engagement but also why clubs, groups, and even gangs exist. By facilitating belongingness in compelling new ways, Facebook, Twitter, and LinkedIn foster digital interactions that change how people can connect and relate to each other today.

The hierarchy of human motivation is just one of many disciplines of psychology that can drive responsive connections today. Another is the psychology of social behavior—a discipline that explains human-to-human interaction. Brands such as Macintosh, TiVo, and Amazon leverage social psychology to elicit positive perceptions from their customers. Specifically, these brands leverage social norms, best appreciated as "rules of thumb."

Psychological research has shown that there are social norms in human communication. These norms guide our expectations and behavior when we interact with others. One example is the norm of politeness. With the politeness norm, it is considered appropriate to use greetings at the start of an exchange, and inappropriate not to do so.

Norms of politeness are so powerful in human interaction that they extend to our interactions with media as well. When leveraged in media, they have a great influence on our perception of brands. Amazon and AOL use words like *Hello* and *Welcome* when we log in. Macintosh greets us with a smile upon startup. TiVo greets us with a smile in every brand communication. By incorporating these simple gestures of politeness, these brands create positive brand perceptions, no matter what the channel.

Engagement and brand perception are key marketing metrics that can be influenced by psychology. But metrics relating to transactions are perhaps most important. Ultimately as marketers, we want our customers to buy something. eBay and Amazon do an excellent job of that. Each produces high-volume and repeated transactions through its interactive storefront. Of the many things these two companies do right, one of the most important is facilitating human judgment and decision making—a discipline in psychology that explains the underpinnings of making choices and taking action.

One of the most interesting findings in human decision making is that people like to make decisions collaboratively. That is, they prefer making decisions with other people instead of by themselves. Collaboration is common for decisions that are as large as home buying and as small as what to have for dinner. Brands such as eBay and Amazon do an outstanding job of fostering collaborative decision making. They allow us to do things like read customer reviews, send product information to our friends for their input, and learn about which other products were purchased by people who purchased what we selected. By permitting interactive collaboration, brands like eBay and Amazon keep customers moving toward their purchase decision. When the design of interactive storefronts parallels our natural decision-making process, the e-commerce brand becomes the central source of decision-making input instead of a peripheral, transactional player. By playing a central role in the decision-making process, brands such as eBay and Amazon help us easily decide to repeatedly do business with them.

Most successful marketing initiatives have psychological underpinnings. For years, some of the most effective marketers have leveraged these principals largely by accident. But use of psychology in marketing doesn't have to be hit or miss. It can become part of your everyday strategic thinking.

CASE STUDY: USING PSYCHOLOGY
TO DIGITALLY DRIVE TOURISM

At Engauge, we recently launched a marketing campaign for the State of Georgia Department of Economic Development. Its goal was to stimulate the Georgia economy through increased tourism and attracting businesses to relocate in Georgia. To accomplish this goal, Georgia had been using several marketing channels to connect with multiple target audiences. These audiences included tourists, businesses, and film producers. Engauge was called in to drive online sign up for a free rewards card that served as an incentive for visiting Georgia attractions.

The rewards card was valuable because it gave visitors to Georgia great perks when they visited state attractions. It was offered to tourists on a multipurpose Georgia Web site that served multiple target audiences. Despite the card's value, there was a problem. Analytics showed that rewards card sign-up rates were low. Ethnographic observation showed that real-world card ownership and usage was low. The Web site creative had recently been refreshed, but the new design had made little impact.

The marketers at the State of Georgia knew that most tourists were not signing up for the rewards card or using it. The problem was they didn't know *why*. To find the answer, we combined traditional market research with psychological insights. Two psychology-driven obstacles to rewards card sign up quickly emerged.

Obstacle 1: Mental Models

The first psychological obstacle to rewards card sign up is best captured by a conversation I recently had with a four-year-old boy named David. I asked David to show me how to drive. David got into my driver's seat and said, "First I put on my seat belt, next I stretch my legs to reach the pedals, then I put my hands on the wheel, and finally I pick up the cell phone and I say, 'Drive, drive!'" David believed that a cell phone was essential equipment for driving. He learned this from his mother, who regularly used her cell phone in the car.

David's perception of how cars work is an example a *mental model*. Mental models describe our perceptions of how things work and guide how we make decisions and behave. They are learned from our experience and direct observation of others. Mental models are powerful and usually help make our lives easier. But sometimes, they can drive behaviors that don't match our expectations.

Marketers run into trouble when their mental models of how customers transact are different from customer models. With this kind of incongruence, the difference between what consumers expect and what marketers offer can stand in the way of transaction.

In the case of Georgia, the tourist mental model for rewards card sign up drove the expectation that the card would be offered on a dedicated Web site for tourists. This mental model was produced because most tourists had visited other state Web sites that were designed this way. With Georgia, however, the card was accessible on a multipurpose Web site geared toward Georgia's multiple audiences. The tourist expectation was so contrary to what people saw on the Georgia Web site that some didn't believe the card was available there even when our researchers told them it was.

Tourists were also convinced that there were fees associated with the rewards card—if not during sign up then certainly during use. The Georgia rewards card had always been free, but tourists had learned to pay for other rewards cards in other states and for other big brands. Past experience set expectations and guided inaccurate mental models of rewards card pricing. Since the Georgia Web site didn't say anything to go against these models, tourists had an inaccurate perception of how the rewards card worked. Ultimately, most tourists didn't sign up for a rewards program that they would have genuinely enjoyed.

To address the mismatch, we reimaged the State of Georgia **iDirect** interactive connection to meet tourist expectations. We created a Web site dedicated exclusively to the rewards card that featured only card-related information. This site also emphasized that the card was free to tourists during both sign up and use. This reimaging created congruence between the mental model of potential tourists and the true state of their world. And this, in turn, drove rewards card transactions.

Obstacle 2: Freezing Behavior

The second psychological obstacle to rewards card sign up is best captured by observing how rats deal with stress and anxiety. During stressful times, like when cats are nearby, rats engage in freezing behavior. Rather than fighting or running away, rats stand still in the presence of cats. Their first line of defense is actually to do nothing. People tend to behave in similar ways, especially when it comes to information overload. Too much information can be stressful and anxiety provoking, causing a kind of paralysis that stands in the way of doing business.

On the existing State of Georgia Web site, tourists were exhibiting freezing behavior, particularly when viewing the home page. The problem was that they were presented with too much information. The brain had to work too hard to learn what to do and how to do it. There was too much detail, and the visual drivers of sign up, like buttons and links, were buried in a sea of other distractions. It was overwhelming, and in reaction many tourists gave up before trying to find what they were looking for.

To address this opportunity, we clustered the information into easily scanned groupings and bulleted separate points into readable form. This helped tourists find and process the key information quickly. We also made visual drivers of behavior more salient by decluttering the background and by using green as the color for buttons that drove card sign up. People who are familiar with traffic systems know that green is associated with a *go* reaction. The design changes to the Georgia Web site made processing the marketing communications far less stressful, freeing the consumer to process the benefits of the rewards card and continue moving forward in the sign up process.

Once the psychological obstacles to card sign up were addressed, sign up rates increased five-fold in comparison with similar months in the previous year. And more importantly, the corresponding real-world card usage along with Georgia tourism increased in turn. By understanding tourist psychology and *why* it was creating obstacles to card sign up, we significantly improved Georgia rewards card membership and Georgia tourism on the whole.

FINAL THOUGHTS

iDirect Marketing and **iBranding** foster a meaningful, interactive conversation with customers that wasn't possible before the advent of a high-speed broadband Internet. In this two-way, multichannel marketing space, an understanding of human psychology is key to making lasting connections with customers. Psychology provides the foundation for making those interactions both natural and profitable.

The future of marketing is about having relevant, meaningful, and seamless digital connections to those you want to influence. It is driven by more than the *how* and the *what* of behavior. It is dependent on understanding the *why*. Most every successful marketing campaign can be explained in retrospect with an understanding of the psychology of consumer behavior. But very few are strategically driven by such an understanding in the planning stage. So open your mind to psychology as a powerful driver of your **iDirect** and **iBranding** marketing results. You'll be glad you did.

Chapter
9

E-Mail Life Support at Home and the Office

Jeanniey Mullen

Executive Chairwoman, E-Mail Experience Council
(eec); Executive Vice President and Chief Marketing
Officer, Zinio and VIVmag LLC; and Coauthor of
Email Marketing: An Hour a Day

A picture is worth a thousand words, so I decided to start off this chapter with a photo of myself to help make a point about how busy our everyday lives have become.

This is me. Not the "crazy me," not the "stressed me," and not even the "Halloween costume" me. This is standard me, at a business conference, sitting in the lobby checking e-mails on my BlackBerry, while I am listening to a voice mail that was e-mailed to me on my laptop and managing a conference call at the same time. Just another "day in the life of a digital executive."

Figure 9.1 Multitasking has become a standard way of business life.

Ten years ago, if people saw this photo, they would think I had lost my marbles. Ten years ago people did not know of the power of **iDirect Marketing**.

Today, however, in a world where, according to the E-mail Experience Council, 50 million people check their e-mail on some type of device before 11:30 in the morning, actions like mine are not odd, they are simply accepted. Over the past two decades, consumer habits have changed. We have become digital addicts. A digital revolution has occurred as we eat, sleep, and breathe.

Where we are today is a phenomenal place—a place where direct marketers can thrive as consumers and prospects actually proactively reach out to marketers, advertisers, and corporations to ask for a relationship. We live in a society where our on-demand lifestyle has made it acceptable to "demand" information and value from the companies we patronize. And, plainly put, there is no cheaper, more effective channel to share information with your consumer than by using e-mail.

HOW TO HARNESS THE POWER OF iDIRECT TO MAXIMIZE YOUR E-MAIL MARKETING EFFORTS

Marketers beware! This chapter is not for the lighthearted. E-mail marketing can be seductively deceptive. Yet leveraging what e-mail can do for you is essential for unleashing the full power of **iDirect Marketing**.

Effective use of e-mail requires much more than sending out a catchy message to an opt-in list. It requires mastering the science of deliverability; the art of creative design; the discipline of multivariant testing (see Appendix); and strategies for integration with other channels. This chapter highlights the key elements you need to understand in order to gain the optimum ROI from your e-mail campaigns.

Step 1: Know What You Are Dealing With

You read e-mail. I read e-mail. That much is certain. But understanding *how* your prospective customers read e-mail is the first step in mastering e-mail success. Less than 60 percent of people who read their e-mail messages read them exclusively on a laptop or PC screen.[1] Digital devices such as the BlackBerry, iPhone, iPod touch, and other Wi-Fi-enabled products provide immediate messaging access 24/7 for consumers and business executives. Scanning, accessing, and taking action on e-mail marketing messages has never been easier, faster, and more convenient.

While it seems that this onslaught of e-mail popularity would be good for marketers, it is often the cause of e-mail's ineffectiveness. Your ease of access is everyone's ease of access. It is what is behind the challenge in capturing the focus and attention of the reader. (If you don't believe me, see my photo at the beginning of this chapter.) Instead of being able to present your company's story or offer information to a person who is focused on nothing else, just the opposite often is true. Your e-mails are scanned, glanced at, and processed with less than 35 percent of the full attention they deserve. This means your message must stand out and be successfully processed to make a connection within milliseconds of being viewed.

Step 2: Understand the Five Key Roles of iDirect E-Mail

In the mid-2000s e-mail moved out of the novelty and early adopter space and into the hardcore direct marketing realm. As a high-response, low-cost alternative to mail or telephones, e-mail became a valued part of the direct marketer's arsenal. Pharmaceutical companies like GlaxoSmithKline began using e-mail to drive trial requests. Catalogers like J.Crew used e-mail to feature and sell products. B-to-B companies like Oracle used e-mail to speed up the sales process for larger purchases. And even online companies like CheapTickets.com relied more and more on e-mail to increase repeat purchases. In the mid-2000s the five key roles of e-mail that now have such an important place in **iDirect** and **iBranding** strategies came into play:

1. *Drive awareness.* E-mails that drive awareness are not your standard "buy it now" e-mails. These e-mails drive a reader to a Web site or store to get them engaged with the brand. Many consumer packaged goods companies use awareness-related e-mails to drive the reader to spend time with their brand. In the example shown in Figure 9.2, Hellmann's mayonnaise uses a sweepstakes

Figure 9.2 An e-mail targeted at driving awareness of a product/promotion.

to get the reader to go to its site. The hope is that you will want to become involved when you land at the site. E-mails such as this one are critical to support a direct relationship with the consumer. According to Forrester,[2] once people enter your e-mail program, they will spend 138 percent more with you than those who do not ever ask for opt-in e-mail permission.

2. *Create ongoing engagement*. Anyone involved with digital marketing knows that the chance of getting someone who has never heard of your company to buy from you right away is close to impossible. This type of direct e-mail helps push ongoing visits to a Web site or store.

Most common in this category are e-newsletters. *Good Morning America* does a fantastic job of sending e-mails (Figure 9.3) that not only inform but encourage you to get interested in past, current, and future topics.

3. *Consideration.* Consideration e-mails are sent when an opt-in Web surfer needs a little push to make a purchase. Travel companies make excellent use of this form of e-mail. Many travel companies drive close to 40 percent of their online revenue this way. Travel companies have seen that people who receive e-mails suggesting travel destinations, pricing, and other related information are up to 60 percent more likely to stay at that hotel than those who did not receive such e-mails periodically. One of my personal favorite consideration e-mails is what I receive from TripAdvisor.

   If you haven't gone to TripAdvisor.com yet, be sure to visit the site. Search for a destination you might want to visit. When it asks you to sign up for e-mails, do so. You will be amazed to see how e-mails from TripAdvisor increase your consideration for travel.

   In addition to providing effective consideration e-mails, TripAdvisor also does a great job of integrating social networking and consumer-generated feedback for its community of believers. An example of the first TripAdvisor e-mail sent out to drive consideration is shown in Figure 9.4.

4. *Drive purchasing.* E-mails that drive purchasing are your hardcore "buy it now" messaging. These are the e-mails that drive the reported $48 ROI touted by the Email Experience Council and Direct Marketing Association. They work well, even in today's e-mail environment where 30 percent of all messages sent to people who expect to be contacted never make it to

Figure 9.3   Example of an e-newsletter.

Figure 9.4 TripAdvisor's e-mails drive consideration.

their inbox. Sears is a company that has mastered the art of successfully using **iDirect** e-mail (Figure 9.5). But keep in mind that one reason these communications from Sears are so effective is that the people reading them know and trust the brand. Sending e-mails that push people to purchase with no prior relationship doesn't work in the world of e-mail marketing,

5. *Retention/cross sell.* This usage takes its cues from the earliest origin of e-mail messaging. When you refer back to the e-mail timeline, you are reminded that

Figure 9.5 Sears uses e-mails to drive immediate purchase.

e-mail became so popular because it was the first digital channel to offer immediate access to enhanced customer service. Retention and cross sell e-mails appear to be focusing on customer service, but actually drive incremental revenue. An example of retention/cross sell e-mails is what you are likely to receive from an airline when you book a flight with it. You will often see messages in your confirmation e-mail asking if you need a hotel or to rent a car. B-to-B marketers also deploy these e-mails well. One example of how IBM does it can be seen in the partial screen shot of one of its e-mails shown in Figure 9.6. IBM has seen e-mail results outperform traditional messaging by double-digit percentages. E-mail is a critical part of its ongoing **iDirect Marketing** strategy.

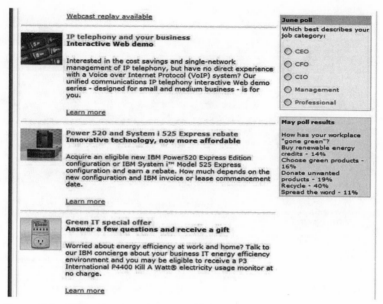

Figure 9.6 IBM uses e-mail to capitalize on relationships and cross-sell.

Step 3: Segment Your E-Mail List to Maximize the Effectiveness of Marketing Directly

In the olden days (aka: last year), many e-mail marketers relied on house-list segments that followed the tried-and-true standard inherited from years of direct marketing practices. Most companies' lists were broken into segments including:

- Best customers (high purchasers, high dollar buyers, or even longtime consumers).
- Worst customers (people on the verge of being removed from the list because of nonresponse).
- New customers (people who often went through a 60–90 day onboarding process to determine what other categories they would fall into).
- Unsubscribes (people who used to be on the list but aren't anymore).

With the new **iDirect** approach, understanding the impact of social media interactions on our targeted e-mail campaigns opens up an entirely new set of segments to leverage.

Now you want to consider how you can split your list, not just by what a targeted person spends, but also by the collective dollars that person influences others to spend (on top of his or her own spending). These new measurement factors reflect the impact of a combination of reach and response.

It might look something like what is shown in Figure 9.7.

In the past, those people who respond marginally, or not at all, to your e-mail campaign were typically the people who you would consider removing from your list. Today though, those people might not individually respond, but they may tell others about your offer, news, or sale. These people could very well turn out to be your best ambassadors and moneymakers.

Step 4: Drive It Home with Creative that Makes an Impact

Understanding when e-mail works best and how to reach the most influential marketing segments are key to getting the **iDirect** results you want. Making your response rates soar is dependent on

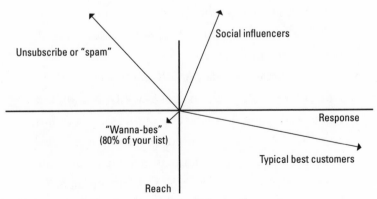

Figure 9.7 Defining the most influential e-mail segments.

your ability to produce impactful creative. The following three tips, taken from my recently published book *Email Marketing: An Hour a Day*, will get you well on your way:

- *Always put new content in context before the user hits "delete."* If your e-mail readers have no context for the message they are reading, your message equity is at risk. In other words, if you send an e-mail to Joe with fresh content and no mental notes for him to refer to (reminders of prior conversations, links, and so on) and Joe scrolls through the e-mail on his BlackBerry while boarding a train to DC, your message equity has dropped to 33 percent or less.

  Conversely, if your message has associated notes (content callouts, links, or other information), you stand a much higher chance of having your message resonate and be responded to by Joe.

- *Link the e-mail's benefits to the reader's long-term goals.* If your e-mail does not clearly and concisely state why the message will help the readers achieve their long-term goals and fulfill future needs, it is at high risk of having low comprehension. A good example might be, "Save this message for when you need to . . ."

  Creating language that is clear and concise, and conveys how your reader will benefit in the long run will pay off many times over.

- *Leverage attention nodes.* An *attention node* is some type of formatting in the e-mail that clearly grabs the reader's attention. In marketing messages, this is most commonly done with a callout box, action tag/button, or other imagery. In text for personal e-mail, attention nodes can be any creative use of spacing or character keys that helps clearly drive where the attention needs to be placed. For example, you can use three asterisks (***) to signify importance.

You will also want to leverage the power of three to succeed. Based on proprietary testing we've done over the past 10 years, three is the optimal number of times you should put a message in front of your readers to maximize clicks. Three is also the number of e-mails new subscribers will read to determine whether they will stay engaged with your brand's e-mail program. And finally, three is the average number of e-mail subscriptions a reader opts into for a given category.

WHY ALL OF THIS MATTERS

You've invested a good bit of time reading about the benefits of e-mail in driving response rates and the key elements to master to make your commitment to e-mail pay off.

The most popular online activities are:

- Searching the Web.
- Finding information for personal use.
- Using Internet e-mail.
- Accessing news and sports information.
- Accessing financial or credit information.

With over 1 *billion* people using e-mail as a regular communication vehicle (many checking in over five times per day), your business cannot afford to do without e-mail in your **iDirect** campaign. You also cannot afford to create a lackluster effort when you roll out the campaign. Remember to test, test, test, test test, test, test, test, test your way to constant improvement, and the stepped up ROI e-mail can deliver for you. Classic direct marketers familiar with the expense of testing direct mail packages remain wary of a one-to-one communication medium with almost unlimited opportunity to test at negligible cost. The brand marketers who never understood or appreciated the value of direct marketing tests in the first place are equally at a loss when it comes to capitalizing on the low cost of e-mail testing. The result is e-mail that generally falls far short of producing at the optimum results that would follow intensive and repetitive testing of all pertinent variables.

The inbox is the beating heart of the Internet—the tightest link ever forged between buyer and seller. E-mail, the only high-volume channel where people opt-in to give marketers permission to send promotions to them, is the powerhouse of digital communication. Whether it is to create awareness, drive purchases, extend relationships, or mobilize a community of activists, e-mail works.

I encourage you to take the gloves off and come out swinging with an e-mail marketing knockout punch. Get bold, get busy, and get messaging. The lowest cost, best targeted advertising and promotion medium you'll encounter in a lifetime is waiting for you. Go **iDirect** with e-mail. Your CFO will be proud of you.

Notes

1. Direct Marketing Association.
2. E-mail Experience Council.
3. Mailer Mailer.
4. OgilvyOne Worldwide.
5. Zinio.
6. Forrester.

Chapter

10

Conversation: What Matters Most for Marketers Now

Joseph Jaffe

Author of *Join the Conversation* and President and Chief
Interruptor of the Marketing Consultancy, crayon

Greg Verdino

Chief Strategy Officer of the
Marketing Consultancy, crayon

L et's begin by stating the obvious: These are challenging times
for marketers.

The traditional media workhorses we once relied upon to do
the heavy lifting for our marketing plans no longer seem quite as

capable of getting the job done. Rising costs, increasingly frag-
mented audiences, and unprecedented clutter combine to make
it more difficult than ever to reach the right people at the right
time in the right place. And even when we do, the odds are that
they won't pay much attention. We rejoice if even 1 percent of
the people on our mailing lists actually respond to an offer. We
judge the success of our television campaigns more by the number of free YouTube views and Twitter mentions they generate
than by the over-the-air impressions we bought.

Speaking of YouTube and Twitter, with the advent of broadband, we have seen social media go mainstream and Web 2.0 technologies dramatically change the dynamics between content
provider and audience. Millions upon millions of people with
Internet-connected computers have the means not only to create
their own content, but also to distribute what they produce to their
own communities of fans and followers who, in turn, are likely to
pass it along and publish their own written, audio, visual, and
video content. As Stan Rapp notes in his Introduction, it's become
a one-to-one-to-everyone world.

We are truly living in a multi-million-channel media universe,
but in no way does it resemble the top-down, broadcast-dominated
environment we accessed while growing up. It is a media landscape
marked by nearly infinite choice and infinite noise. The brands that
garner the most attention are not the ones whose ads travel down
fiber optics to captivate a loyal viewing audience, but the ones
whose stories travel from consumer to consumer—on their blogs,
in their tweets, in YouTube videos, and on Facebook profiles.

We see our world changing and know we need to change too.
But most marketers stay inside a familiar comfort zone and for
the most part stick with the same old brand advertising and direct
marketing approaches. Is it any wonder then that so many marketers find it simply too difficult to achieve the results they need
to survive and thrive in these challenging times? Failure has

become more common than success in today's bewildering marketing scene.

WHAT WE HAVE HERE IS
A FAILURE TO COMMUNICATE

Perhaps it would be more accurate to say we have a failure of communications.

Marketing communication as we know it—from direct mail and print, to television and, yes, digital advertising online as well—represents the status quo. It is media-dependent, generally one way, and increasingly falls short in an interconnected Web 2.0 environment. Sure, now and then a campaign rises above the clutter to drive awareness, get people talking, and generate desired results, but the impact is fleeting. As soon as the campaign ends—the last ad runs, the last consumer opens the last envelope—there is a disconnect. What was the call to action, if any? What has been done to start an ongoing conversation?

The usual answer (and it isn't a very good one) is turn to: "Another campaign, another attempt to break through, another big media spend, another switch to another agency." With the CEO pressuring the CMO for measurable results right now, it's an answer that doesn't sit very well. In fact, it bears a striking resemblance to Albert Einstein's definition of insanity: doing the same thing over and over again, expecting different results.

WHAT DOES REAL CHANGE LOOK LIKE?

In Joseph Jaffe's book *Join the Conversation* and at our marketing consultancy crayon, we advocate doing things differently so that our clients can achieve different results. For us, "conversation" is the difference maker—for marketers, it is a concept that stands in stark contrast to traditional modes of communication. We see strategically sound conversational executions working exception-ally well—even in a plunging economy. They often serve as the driving force within a cohesive **iDirect** or **iBranding** marketing solution.

We advise our clients to move beyond the tried and true by tap-ping into the power of community, dialogue, and partnership—and by adopting new approaches that are inherently two way, usually media-independent, and by definition participatory rather than passive. To do so requires a fluency in social media and Web 2.0 technology, along with an understanding that these tools and technologies have granted consumers an unprecedented level of influence over the marketing process. Consumers now hold com-panies they choose to do business with to a higher standard. As marketers, we have much to gain by earning the trust and atten-tion of these "influentials."

Nowadays, we're not the only voice preaching this particular gospel. If you are a reader of the industry trades or mainstream business magazines, you've no doubt seen numerous articles that urge marketers to follow the insight first offered by Joseph years ago to "join the conversation." You are told to add social media to your integrated plan, embrace social marketing or digital word of mouth, and define new go-to-market strategies for connecting with an "in control" consumer.

It's not difficult to buy in to the concept of conversational mar-keting. It sounds like common sense and seems like a logical means of countering the triple threat of rising media costs, shrink-ing mass media audiences, and hard-to-measure results.

Yet, for all the conversation about conversation, most compa-nies actually do little or nothing to change their ways. They con-tinue spending a small fortune on the diminished effectiveness of the traditional media that consumers have long since stopped tak-ing seriously. Far too many companies resist inevitable change and continue doing more or less the same as always—all the while bemoaning the fact that what they are doing no longer does what it once did.

Other marketers superficially experiment with a laundry list of new tools—they set-up their Twitter accounts, create Facebook fan pages, upload branded videos to YouTube, and launch corporate blogs. They are quick to chase the latest shiny "next thing" and just as quick to abandon it when another new thing comes along. At the end of the day, they've managed to check a number of boxes on their innovation checklist, while the ground keeps shifting under them.

The bad news is that you may see your organization in the scenarios described above. The good news is that, even if you do, you have a tremendous opportunity to rise above the pack—provided you are ready, willing, and able to embrace change. But you'll need to come to terms with the fact that *joining the conversation* isn't a minor matter anymore; it's the key element of a successful **iBranding** or **iDirect** marketing outcome when hundreds of millions of people access social media every day.

The rise of social networking has put conversation in the spotlight. However, to keep things in perspective, we know that this aspect of consumer behavior is far from new. People have always had conversations about your company, brand, or products.

IF EVERYTHING OLD IS NEW AGAIN, WHAT HAS CHANGED?

Years ago, buyer/seller conversations happened face to face or over the phone, between two individuals or among small groups. If buzz spread, it spread slowly, a few people at a time. Today, those conversations take place on blogs, forums, and message boards. Consumers spread messages and stories about your product or service and how what you sold them performed by creating Facebook groups, by making and uploading Web videos, and by injecting your brand name into their Twitter messages. It is now a matter of what is said and how far and how quickly word will spread, more than a matter of whether your product or service will be talked about at all. The social Web is tightly wired for consumer-to-consumer transmission of shared opinions and, fact is, online conversations about your brand are happening right now with your participation or not.

The question we'd like to pose is this: Wouldn't you want your brand to participate, to know what its fans and foes are saying, to have a voice in the conversation, to express its own beliefs, and even defend itself as necessary?

We knew you'd say "yes," so what follows is some practical advice about how to get started. Specifically, we talk about how you can get into the game and make conversational imperatives a strategic part of each and every marketing plan you implement.

GET IN THE GAME

As the old saying goes, "You've gotta be in it to win it." Every conversational marketing strategy begins with a few simple steps that will provide the foundation for everything you do. These steps are not just for moments of crisis—after a prominent blogger writes a scathing review, after an angry crowd generates an explosion in Twitter activity, after a bad customer experience gains exposure through a widely shared YouTube video. Of course, you can turn to conversational marketing to navigate these *shark*-infested waters, but that is not enough. By establishing your cyber credibility in advance and earning the respect of savvy Web-oriented consumers who are well versed in the conversational lifestyle online, you gain profitable allegiance whether or not a crisis situation ever arises.

Here are three practical, easy-to-execute, first steps that any company—from the scrappiest start-up to the largest blue chip multinational—can take:

- *Start listening to the conversation.* Set up Google alerts and Twitter search feeds for your company name, brand and product names, your Web site URLs, and the names of your key executives. You might want to create alerts to be informed about your competitors and business category too. While you can certainly invest in more sophisticated monitoring services, this step alone is enough to equip you with the input necessary to understand who is talking and what they're saying. You'll get to know your most vocal supporters and your harshest critics, and you'll set the stage for your own participation in the ongoing dialogue about your brand and other relevant topics.

- *Join the consumer's communities.* While creating branded accounts on Facebook, Twitter, YouTube, and Flickr should never be mistaken for strategy, securing your brand names (and variations thereof) and establishing a series of distributed hubs are important steps in getting started. These hubs will provide you with a presence in the communities where consumer conversations are most likely to happen, will give you natural outlets for branded content, and will create opportunities to aggregate permission-based communities of your own, populated with those people interested in what you have to offer.

- *Become an active conversationalist.* If the first two steps provide you with an understanding of which conversations you might want to join and some places to plant your own seeds of conversation, your next logical step is to begin actively participating. Respond where appropriate, introduce your own topics of conversation, provide value to influencers interested in engaging directly with you, and motivate actions leading to a sale online or offline (an **iDirect** fundamental). Begin aggregating members of your brand's community and find ways to embrace and empower the consumers who, themselves, bring together communities of people who might be interested in what you have to offer. Above all, do these things in ways that are both true to who you are and the values of your brand, and respectful of the interests and standards of the online communities you're joining.

Sometimes, you'll find that a simple approach delivers squarely for your objectives. For example, Comcast and JetBlue—both in the wake of major social media firestorms ignited by consumers who experienced poor service—recognized the need to dial into the conversation and provide superior customer support in real time. Today, they deliver this promise with support-oriented Twitter accounts (at comcastcares and jetblue, respectively) that make it easy for them to gather feedback, listen for service issues, and connect directly with customers in need of help or advice.

Other times, your business challenges point toward more robust social media strategies. When Ford Motor Company wanted to shift perception of its brand and vehicles, it rolled out an integrated conversational marketing strategy that includes not only an active distinctly human Twitter presence and a series of distributed social media hubs, but also several key programs that literally put their latest vehicles in the hands of key influencers. One recent promotion for the 2010 Fiesta let 100 bloggers "own" vehicles for a full year in return for their participation in a series of activities and content creation opportunities, while another offered week-long SUV loans to bloggers planning short road trips. Clearly, Ford understands that if you truly want to shift perception, there is no better way than to demonstrate that you really are a thought leader and tastemaker who has the social platforms necessary to spread the word to consumers.

In each case outlined here, the brand identified a marketing challenge by listening to the conversation already happening, got in the game by establishing a presence in the right social media channels, and made appropriate commitments to participating in existing and new conversations about its companies and products in ways that not only benefit the brands but also provide value to consumers.

COMMIT TO CONVERSATION

If you just take our advice to get in the game and stop there, you already will be better off than the vast majority of marketers out there. However, if you do nothing more than get in the game, you might be disappointed with your results.

We've been saying this to our clients for years, yet it bears repeating: Marketing is a commitment, not a campaign. Conversation is an always-on phenomenon. There is no end date to it. The content that consumers create about your brand (good, bad, and otherwise) has the potential to live forever in cyberspace and is always just a Google search away from anyone's fingertips. What's more—thanks to the emergence of newer social platforms like Twitter, life-streaming tools like FriendFeed, Posterous, and Tumblr, and live video-streaming services like Ustream and Justin.tv—online conversations now take place in real time.

Your brand can be built up or burnt down in the "now." It is the consumer—not your company—who decides what happens next. One of the most important things you can do—for your customers and also for your brand—is to maintain a committed, long-term presence that allows you to be accepted into the target consumer's or business customer's daily life online and to offer helpful experiences and ideas that are both proactive and reactive.

At crayon we call this process *commitment to conversation*, and it is a process. It covers the gamut from initiating influencer outreach to monitoring the conversation that ensues; from under-standing when and how to join in constructive debate (and avoid destructive arguments) to having a ready-made contingency plan for when something goes wrong; from course correction to stok-ing positive vibes so that they last longer and are heard more often.

If consumers are always on through social media, then you must be too. Yes, we really do mean 365 days per year—and while near-term ROI is not out of the question, your focus should remain squarely on long-term ROR (return on relationship). This requires an understanding of lifetime value and customer relationship management intrinsic to an **iDirect** and **iBranding** point of view. You will also need both patience and an investment in human resources—a move that will still be providing bottom-line bene-fit long after your current TV campaign has been forgotten.

EMBED CONVERSATION IN YOUR MARKETING STRATEGY

At this stage of the digital revolution, it may seem that conversa-tional marketing and social media marketing are one and the same. They're not. While it would be difficult to maintain a com-mitment to conversation without making effective use of social media tools, it would be foolish to think of conversation as just another channel in your marketing mix or, even worse, a silo that stands apart from your overall holistic media strategy.

To put it another way: Conversation is not a place, and social is not a site.

It might be possible to envision a not-so-distant future when the entire Web—not just the sites we classify as social media today—is infused with conversation. We already see media destinations as diverse as CNN and World Wrestling Entertainment incorporat-ing community functionality, social tools, consumer-generated content, and shared functionality. More than a few big brands manage online social networks designed specifically for their customers and fans. Dell has become famous for groundbreaking initiatives like IdeaStorm.com and DigitalNomads.com, while fans of the Segway electric two-wheelers can connect at social.segway.com, and consumers interested in all things "high definition" can meet other like-minded individuals at Panasonic's LivinginHD.com. Facebook Connect, and Google Connect make it easy to find and engage with your online connections across hundreds of sites that have no formal affiliation with Facebook or Google. These pace-setters of the digital content revolution are in essence laying the groundwork for a social Web operating system that allows you to take friends along with you wherever you go online.

The rise to prominence of social interaction online in an amazingly short time highlights a basic fact of human nature. Social networking is not a place where we hang out; social is what we are no matter where we happen to be.

This is even true if we happen to be in front of the TV or the mailbox. Think about the average DR TV spot or the call-out on the envelope of a direct mail package. Both are built to start conversations between a marketer and the prospect. Both make brand-building impressions as well as presenting a powerful offer designed to get a response (See Chapter 4: Lucas Donat's Direct Goes Emotional with New iDTV Advertising). The consumer responds, beginning a permission-based dialogue by mail or online that might last through a single exchange or that might last a lifetime depending on what the marketer does to continue the conversation.

However, at a time when Internet access is nearing ubiquity, **iDirect** conversations increasingly are fueled by social media and consumer expectations. It's now critical that we infuse conversational thinking into everything we do and find better, smarter ways to make use of Web 2.0 tools built from the ground up for conversation.

While we can't write your conversational strategy without a full briefing on your marketing situation, we can share one key to approaching conversation with your customers from a strategic standpoint: Be sure to focus on how people behave, not the tools they use.

There are dozens of popular social media platforms, each with its own vibrant community of passionate users. If you were so inclined, you could try a new service practically every day of the year and still miss out on a number of new, cutting-edge sites. As a twenty-first–century marketer, you might feel an almost unbearable urge to try new things, or you might be paralyzed by the sheer number of choices. Then again you might do a little bit of everything (none of it well) or you might do nothing at all.

Succumb to the former, and you'll end up with a batch of disjointed tactics in search of a strategy. Settle for the latter, and you run the risk of being left behind, if not by your competitors then surely by your customers.

The good news is that choosing the right technology of the moment doesn't really matter. Some of the social platforms we've already mentioned might be out of business by the time you read this book, but the behaviors they empower and which, in turn, fuel the site's intense popularity will endure. It's the behaviors that count.

One of the most important things you can do is understand why and how consumers are participating in the various forms of social networking and find the right way not only to join in but also to improve that experience. Just as conversations are never one-sided, neither is conversational marketing only about relevant engagement. When approached strategically, within the reinvented **iDirect** and **iBranding** framework, it is a direct path to winning an emotional brand connection and a measurable increase in profitable business.

Think of conversation with desired prospects and core customers not just "in and of itself," but as a means to an end. By getting in the game and committing to value-based engagement with the right people, you are showing you care and are giving them reason to take your brand into their lives. It is the antithesis of intrusive advertising. By improving your game, as you learn by trial and error how to guide the conversation, you can turn customers into ambassadors who share your brand story with their personal friends and online network connections.

Driving actions that build your brand and deliver tangible results is what this chapter and this book are all about. It's time to wholeheartedly *join the conversation*. Leave the competition in the dustbin of advertising history while you partner with your customer community in the new win-win era of **iBranding** and **iDirect Marketing**.

Chapter
11

iDirect Marketing at Best Buy for Business

Janet Rubio

Chief Insights Officer, Engauge

Being recognized as one of the greatest retail brands, a place just about everybody has shopped, is not the best starting point for reaching out to the business market. In fact, it's easy to imagine why business customers may be dubious about that retailer becoming the best choice for them.

After all, the needs of consumers are different from those of businesses.

Consumers use their own money and have full decision-making authority over how to spend it. Businesses usually have a budget and approval process. Consumers frequently make impulse purchases. Businesses plan their purchases well in advance.

Consumers want choices and bargains. Businesses want value and service. Indeed, there is a world of difference.

Best Buy has some of the smartest marketers employed at its Minnesota headquarters. It was obvious that if B-to-B needs are different, then the marketing must be different as well.

Fortunately, just at the time that Best Buy set about greatly expanding its share of the business market, the powerful new **iDirect** dynamic was beginning to take hold. Look at what was now possible in an interconnected business environment: innovative online customer relationships, tremendous search engines for prospecting, easy and safe e-commerce, social networking, and access to fresh behavioral data. While Web 2.0 was heavily consumer-oriented, the marketers at Best Buy felt strongly that the evolving Internet meeting place held great promise for B-to-B lead generating and budding customer relationships.

The challenge for Best Buy for Business (BBFB) was simple yet massive. How do we build a marketing ecosystem that takes advantage of accountable data-driven practices while capitalizing on the power of the Internet to gain cost efficiencies and a targeting advantage? In short, how do we make **iDirect Marketing** pay off for a B-to-B marketer?

Engauge Direct was selected by Best Buy for Business to help meet the challenge. We began working with one of those outstanding BBFB marketers mentioned earlier, John Samuels, the director of business-to-business marketing. John and his team were responsible for successful penetration of the business market and developing the marketing tools required to make it happen.

We began by defining how to best serve the customers' needs. We believed that if we kept the customer at the center of everything and never lost sight of providing added value, we would make the right decisions.

The first step was to apply the proprietary "share of pocketbook" platform to gain a clear understanding of the budget each customer in each category had available and how much of it was spent with BBFB. We knew that if Company A had a $10,000 budget but only spent $1,000 of it with us, that we were still in an early stage of winning that customer over. On the other end of the spectrum, if Company B had $1,500 in budget accounts and spent $1,000 with us, then we could count that customer as a loyal buyer. There was the same amount of revenue to us but a very different customer outlook. At the same time, Company B was in a category with far more growth potential than Company A. Another significant factor within the prospect's category was the *potential* within the category. Depending upon how the algorithm worked out, our approach would be quite different for each targeted company.

BUILDING A DATA MART FOR HYPERGROWTH IN THE DIGITAL ERA

BBFB had a lot of data but they were in many disparate silos. There was value in each database within the company, but there was no easy access for an overview of any single customer behavior or even of a group of customers.

This might seem surprising given the size of Best Buy and its marketing muscle. Actually, though, it's not. Many of the best-known B-to-B companies in the world struggle to comprehend the mountains of data they have accumulated.

Think of it this way. BBFB has transaction details going back for years from multiple channels, for thousands of products, from hundreds of thousands of customers, with ever-changing new information. And, of course, in any B-to-B environment there are going to be multiple decision makers and a multifaceted approval process. It's enough to make your head spin. But to turn B-to-B data into profitable sales, a single, functional, easily accessible, and actionable data mart had to be built:

- We needed a *data mart system* that supported transactional information, relationship segment information, channel information, and promotional information. There had to be a full 360 degree view into the business life of the customer if we were going to be successful.

- We needed an *analytic and reporting environment* providing a constantly updated view of customers and prospects. We knew this was the only way to ensure that our spending levels were appropriate to the potential at any given time and that our messaging would be relevant.

- We needed to *test communication* formats, frequencies, copy appeals, and offers as well as media channels to be certain we were optimizing ROI.

- We needed a fully *integrated customer contact system* recognizing that customers may talk to or buy from field sales reps, phone reps, retail stores, or online. We wanted to capitalize on the strengths of each channel and have a multichannel snapshot of each customer's performance.

In the end, our goal could be simply stated: Grow the customer base and its spending level while minimizing the cost to motivate actions to make it happen.

Because we expected that success was going to come from fairly small businesses with relatively small budgets, we determined that the only way to achieve our goal was to leverage the cost efficiencies of the Internet along with the tried-and-true tactics of addressable direct marketing. In short, Direct + Digital = **iDirect Marketing** solutions.

The marketing battleground for customers' minds and wallets has moved to the Internet. Without the digital data provided where business lives today, we would never get past square one.

Our customers go online for their news, their product information, their sourcing searches, their view of competitors, and almost everything else they want to know. The Web represents a massive new source of data about who our customers are and what is important to them. Companies who figure out the best new way to capture that information, transform it into meaningful insights, and take appropriate action are the clear winners in the future.

DRIVING SEGMENTED PROGRAMS WITH ANALYTIC STREAMING

Back in the long-ago 1990s, a marketing database contained summary fields that allowed you to select and count names and addresses. Large-scale databases were housed on big iron running Oracle. To perform any type of analysis, you had to extract data sets and put them into an analytic software package such as SAS. Getting to the information entailed a significant and costly body of work.

Today we have super fast servers storing massive amounts of easily accessed data. Most B-to-B databases run on those servers. And we have analytic and data mining tools on our desktop that can bring up what's needed for real-time decision making. The keys to the kingdom are at our fingertips.

For BBFB we developed a series of data cubes that we could compare with each other. Imagine a Rubik's cube where you can twist and turn customer information and view it from many different perspectives. We looked at buying patterns, types of products initially purchased compared to what was bought later, the favored channels, the interval between purchases, and a firmographic description of the customer.

We utilized our own proprietary tool, CORE, to score the potential budget size each customer had available to spend and how much of it we were capturing.

BBFB focused on two primary goals:

- Determine sizable customer segments that had meaningful differences in past behavior and buying power. If we could accomplish this, we knew we could develop powerful, relevant communications that would deliver strong ROIs against each profile.
- Create a reliable system for leveraging the data to generate a steady flow of quality leads at acceptable cost.

BBFB ultimately ended up with seven discreet groups for modeling predictive behavior and optimizing sales force performance.

TESTING TO FIND THE OPTIMAL CHANNEL MIX

Now armed with a fully defined database ecosystem, we moved on to testing how best to communicate with each of the profiled segments.

BBFB tried various combinations of direct mail, e-mail, and phone calls to 250,000 customers and prospects in various testing segments. This was a carefully structured effort designed to understand which combination of connection points produced the best results.

One segment received a direct mail piece. Another segment received the direct mail piece followed up by an e-mail contact. A third segment received one direct mail piece and two e-mails, and a fourth segment got three e-mails. All the segments contained a subset that also received a follow-up phone call. And, of course, we also had a control group that received the usual monthly e-mail communications.

The copy was as customized as the data would allow with personalization used in multiple places within each communication. The mail piece included a page of stickers that could easily be detached by the targeted prospect. Recipients were encouraged to place the stickers anywhere that would be visible around the office. BBFB field sales representatives were empowered to offer special discounts to any business with stickers on display when they dropped by the office.

The BBFB internal customer relationship management (CRM) system alerted the sales team to make reps aware of their role in the campaign. Results were quite revealing. All the cells that received a follow-up phone call showed an elevated positive ROI. The campaign to prospects that received the direct mail piece and more than one e-mail but no phone call broke even. The group that received the e-mails alone also broke even. The bottom line in this instance was that, in a B-to-B marketing world, personal contact turned out to be the key. The far more costly sequence including the elaborate direct mail piece did not bring a greater response than the group that only received the three e-mails.

In short, for this test campaign, most of the prospect and customer dialog moved to the phone center and the Internet. Direct mail will always retain a role in the mix, but its former dominance of B-to-B communication is at an end.

PUTTING IT ALL TOGETHER IN A FULLY INTEGRATED CONTACT SYSTEM

John Samuels (the director of business-to-business marketing) felt we were now ready to move into locking down communication streams for each segment. BBFB wanted the following:

- Timing and pace of contacts for consistent motivation and measurable profitability.
- Communications that would be relevant and informative.
- Message mix to both sell products and build relationships.

- Cross selling or up selling existing customers based on their current buying behavior.
- Support the sales forces' lead requirement.

We crafted several imaginative communication formats and versioned messaging and frequency by segment. Each segment also had some unique contacts planned for it. We laid out timing and budgets for a year. Smart stuff, but fairly straightforward. At least that's how it appears until you look under the hood at the underlying dynamics to see how far we, as **iDirect** marketers, have come in a relatively short time.

Think back to the old days again, the 1990s, and think about what sales rep lead generation was like then. That's when we started by assembling a list to make outbound phone calls. On the calls the phone rep would get to the usual questions: Are you in the market to buy? What do you value most in the product? What is your time frame? What is your budget? We would then take those answers and feed them to the sales force as A, B, or C leads. Sound familiar?

Okay, now think about what BBFB built a decade later. Via the data mart ecosystem, we know who is in the market to buy because our analytic tools allow us to predict it. We know what kinds of products they are likely interested in based on what they have bought in the past as well as what others who resemble them have bought. We know the time frame based on their past buying history. And via CORE scoring, we also know what information to make readily available when they need to access it. In effect, our segments have become surrogates for far more sophistication than the "old" ABC designation allowed. Quite powerful.

You might think that in an **iDirect** world the contact center would play a diminished role. After all, if the Web is the center of the universe and customers are using it to outmaneuver competitors, aren't human beings on the telephone dispensable? No, they're not. Remember that for B-to-B it's all about service and personal communication which is best delivered by dedicated people. Just because the marketing environment is shifting, don't assume that basic human needs have changed.

Imagine what BBFB is able to do when all the phone salespeople are given data-driven virtual scripts for up sell and cross sell. Think about the impact of the Amazon consumer up sell model in the hands of trained B-to-B qualifiers and closers on a phone! And think about what it can mean to transfer some of the costly administration of the sale away from phone rep and back to the Web!

Data warehouses will continue to store more multichannel customer behavior. Data management/CRM tools will make all of this knowledge more accessible. Reconstituted contact centers will continue to flourish. By utilizing the new tool set, a phone rep can know the answers to the traditional "W" questions before he or she answers or dials the phone. Who. What. When. Where. Closing rates and average order values go up. Customer retention and satisfaction improves. Sales force turnover is reduced as commissions are sure to increase.

BBFB developed a system that integrates sales and marketing, while reducing the cost of the sale. We created a system that moves far beyond traditional B-to-B targeting based on SIC codes and employee size. It is a system that combines the best of direct marketing practices with the power of the Web.

SO WHAT'S NEXT?

Look for more Web behavior data to be fused with offline buying behavior data. Customers will be exposed to more relevant information as a result, and marketers will see a lower selling cost and higher customer retention rate.

Look for more innovation around social networking in B-to-B environments. More business marketers will be maintaining an online conversation with their customers. The hottest trends in today's consumer marketing will migrate to business marketing.

And finally, look for Best Buy for Business to become a recognized leader in the small business market! The possibilities of what can be done with the data management system it created are endless.

Just some of what can be expected:

- Scripting cross sell and up sell scenarios so they maximize the value of their customers and capture more of their budgets.
- Developing product bundles or offers based on affinities in the data.
- Crafting highly relevant, personalized microsegmented messages.
- Defining sales quotas based on the unrealized revenue potential in the various value segmentation models.
- Defending high-value customers against competitive attacks.
- Creating product sales roadmaps by channel based on a new understanding of media channel budget allocation.

What an exciting time to be a B-to-B **iDirect** marketer!

Chapter
12

iBrands: The New Face of the Consumer

Michael McCathren

Conversation Catalyst, Chick-fil-A, Inc.

For decades *brand equity* has been the term used by companies, their shareholders, and investment bankers to represent the value of a particular brand in the marketplace. The more an ad agency's creative, a product's improvement, or the company's customer relationship management added to a brand's equity, the better. From generation to generation, little changed in that marketing mantra.

When Web 1.0 arrived, brands began vying for consumer awareness in cyberspace. Before long just about every business was in the business of saying great things about itself online. In return, an increasing number of consumers found themselves interacting with brands in strange new ways. Then a new wave of Web 2.0

digital technology caused the most dramatic break with the past since the emergence of mass production and mass marketing almost a century ago.

John Blossom in *Content Nation,* the classic work on social media, says, "When the fundamental power of any one person to exert an influence over almost any other person on the planet changes, a tool with great scalability emerges that will exert a change on the future . . . as surely as language itself changed our humanness."

Consumers suddenly were no longer just about consuming: With high-speed broadband access, consumers became producers. The ease of doing your own thing online with electronic publishing gives individuals a global voice for sharing their stories, their favorite food or music, career happenings, family news, opinions about products or customer service (including yours), and doing almost anything else imaginable. What drives much of this interpersonal communication is the human need to enhance one's importance and "belong" to the tribe when interfacing with old and new friends. We are all content producers. We also are followers of other content producers.

Your customers busily peck away at the computer keyboard to create their personal Internet brand, an **iBrand** of their own, with its own set of brand equity components. The winning marketers of tomorrow will know how to raise the value of their customers' Internet equity. Increasingly, in order to build your own brand identity, you must know what makes an influential consumer's **iBrand** tick. Practitioners of **iDirect Marketing** will be increasingly able to join their customers in a reciprocal brand-building experience. *One-to-one* marketing has become *Brand-to-iBrand* marketing.

Let's look at how this new perception of the brand-building process applies to a few of the traditional brand equity components.

iBRANDS CREATE CONTENT

There's something in human nature that drives us to create. Individuals from every walk of life from our first kindergarten crayon-drawing experience into our adult years enjoy self-expression. Whether something tangible is created or it's an innovative way to get something done or simply sharing a point of view, there's satisfaction in making a statement that enlarges a person's sphere of influence. This basic human attribute now intersects with the extraordinary interactive **iBrand** opportunities made possible by the new social media and advanced digital technology.

One way to help consumers build their **iBrands** as producers is to give them the right raw materials. Just as manufacturers need a supply chain, consumer **iBrands** require raw materials to spark the motivation to create. At Chick-fil-A, we have been, and continue to be, the beneficiaries of a brilliant, once-in-a-brand's-lifetime advertising phenomenon. The cow campaign, which began as a billboard program over 12 years ago, has evolved into a hotbed of **iBranding** activities to spark the creativity of Chick-fil-A believers. They print their own online messages on the cow's sandwich board, put cow spots on just about anything, collect one-of-a-kind Chick-fil-A plush cows, including outfits and accessories for the cuddly toys. They'll stand in line under a hot sun to get their picture taken with the cow and share the photos with friends and family on Flickr.

For our **iBranding** consumers, the cow campaign provides raw materials on which they can put their own personal stamp of ownership. Then they share this creation with their marketsphere hoping for positive comments or, better yet, reuse as recycled raw material for other people to invent their own **iBrands**. When that happens, the originator's personal **iBrand** equity gets a huge boost. As a result, the Chick-fil-A brand also does well because the more we increase our customer's **iBrand** equity, the deeper our heritage becomes embedded at the top of that person's share of mind.

Beyond what the marketer can achieve with awareness advertising, the face-to-face experience provides what only an **iBrand** can do for you. This is where most of today's brand marketers fall flat. In recent years marketing executives have slowly poisoned their own brand identity by forgetting that in this digital age it's the experience that defines brand value far more than the advertising. Today more than ever, marketers need to realize that the shortest route to building the business lies in building value for each consumer's **iBrand** in cyberspace. It means giving consumers something special to talk about through a one-of-a-kind product-related or service-related experience. When product parity in almost every industry is at an all-time high, it's unique, caring surprises worthy of a tweet, a blog mention, or a text message that earn **iBranding** points for your brand.

About six years ago Chick-fil-A founder, Truett S. Cathy (http://www.truettcathy.com), began a new movement within Chick-fil-A that was unheard of in the fast food industry (fast "rude" industry in some circles at that time). He set an example for his employees by showing every customer how genuinely appreciative he was that customers would select Chick-fil-A over all the other choices out there. He conveyed that serving them was sincerely a pleasure by replying to every "thank you" with a "my pleasure." Truett believed that all people should be treated with honor, dignity, and respect no matter who they are, what they do, where they come from, or where they choose to eat. It didn't take long before the customer stories began to spread about what an impression just the simple act of saying "my pleasure" was making on a customer's fast food experience. Comments such as "It made my day," "What a pleasant surprise," and "I truly felt appreciated" came streaming in. Nowadays, our brand benefits by the speed with which such positive comments travels on the Internet.

Chick-fil-A has won many awards for its customer service including "Customer Service Champs"[1] and the "Choice in Chains" Customer Satisfaction Award (chicken category) for 14 out of the last 15 years. Although these accolades are a nice confirmation that our service philosophy has gained tangible results, what's most important is how this has transformed the customer experience. There is a big social media payoff in today's Internet-dependant world: Offline experiences have become a gold mine of raw material that consumers draw upon in producing online content that adds value to their **iBrand** equity and, at the same time, to our own.

It is much easier nowadays for stories of amazing service to contribute to your brand equity because sharing those experiences is now intrinsic to the i-life of the consumer's own brand. When an interesting, out-of-context experience is shared online, members of a cyberspace subculture community become aware of something the general public doesn't get yet. You have conveyed what it feels like to be truly appreciated as a customer, the warm feeling you have when a stranger (a teenage stranger at that—with no obligation to do anything for you beyond what the hourly position requires), honestly wants to do everything for you. It's a sad commentary on society when experiences like these are more the exception than the rule. But a service renaissance is brewing, and its source is the small bits of raw material that consumer **iBrands** experience and call to the attention of others. Some company brands will see the light at the end of these customer service dark ages and become the DaVincis of customer satisfaction. Others will attempt to contribute to the ongoing digital conversation— only to become the victim of their own heritage of poor service as Web 2.0 consumers build their **iBrands** by tearing down those product and service companies that disappoint.

True Story: Customer E-Mail Message: I just wanted to let you know this establishment is PERFECT! I frequent your location for lunch, and the food is always great, hot, and fresh. The establishment is always very clean. Most of all, the employees are always extremely nice! What a refreshing change in the fast-food environment. I have always been impressed with how efficient this location is—it's always super busy during the lunch hour, but I have never waited long to get my order taken or food service. When I have sat down inside to eat, I am often impressed by the helpfulness of your staff— helping mothers gather their items needed when also trying to handle their babies, helping people get napkins and condiments when their hands are full, refilling drinks, etc. They go above and beyond. Other fast food places need to take note, because you guys are doing it all (the) right ways!

This is the typical theme we hear from many of our customers. Note that it wasn't the advertising being talked about, the cows, the great, hot and fresh food, or the cleanliness that made this "refreshing" experience different from other fast-food encounters. It was the extremely nice employees. But wait. Is employee hiring and training a marketing responsibility? No, but marketing is one of its beneficiaries. Increasing **iBrand** equity has to be an enterprisewide strategy. Operations, manufacturing, sales, distribution, and customer service are all contributors.

Another way the marketer's brand can support the consumer's **iBrand** content production is to provide a marketsphere for what is being produced. How can a brand create such a market? First, you need a clear picture of just what the consumer's **iBrand** is busily establishing about itself. Understanding attitudes and behaviors of customers doesn't necessarily require an expensive research project. It could be as simple as becoming a follower of your most influential **iBranded** customers and observing what they produce. It may be an active blog, a streaming Twitter, or great Facebook page. As these cyber citizens create, they reveal a great deal about themselves.

Say a customer Twitters about her experiences with your brand, and her current marketsphere is 20 followers. If a brand responded by inviting her to visit its branded online space, such as its Facebook fans page, where a marketsphere of tens of thousands of like-minded users congregate, she would likely find people interested in reading what she has to say. It could represent a sizable contribution to her **iBrand** equity and the number of followers attracted to her digital identity.

It's an interesting example of the "content product" coming from one **iBrand** becoming the raw material of another. Let's say a blogger with a couple of hundred subscribers reads the Twitter post mentioned above. That Twitter post (her product, the blogger's raw material) sparks a new blog post that leads to hundreds of people learning about her amazing customer service experience. That's the beauty of **iBranding** and word-of-mouth marketing in the new millennium; something traditional advertising will never do.

To grow your brand, give your **iBrand** followers something positive, unique, and interesting to talk about and an expanded marketsphere with which to share it, and they'll keep coming back to you for more raw material.

iBRANDS CREATE LOYALTY

Now that customers are fashioning their own personal brands, let's look more closely at the similarities between how customer **iBrands** function and the way a traditional business or product brand operates.

I like how Gareth Kay begins to draw connections between the marketer's brand and people as brands. In *The Age of Conversation* Gareth wrote, "What makes people, and brands, worthy of conversation is their ability to possess a different combination of qualities that appeal to different people at different times. They [**iBrands**] are multi-faceted, full of depth and nuance. A brand [**iBrand**] worthy of long-term conversation needs to constantly change the way it [he or she] expresses itself and generates a coherent stream of actions that flow from its [his or her] point of view on the world." (Bracketed inserts added by me.)

Loyalty can be established in several ways. Figure 12.1 demonstrates the process.

Consumer **iBrands** follow the same curve as a company's traditional brand, from being unknown online to having significant influence with a large number of people (followers, readers, subscribers, visitors, etc.). A potential customer can be virtually unknown until she decides to post a comment on your brand's Facebook fans page or makes the first entry about you in her blog. Even at that point she's still relatively unknown because she has no followership. Based on the nature of her comment, you

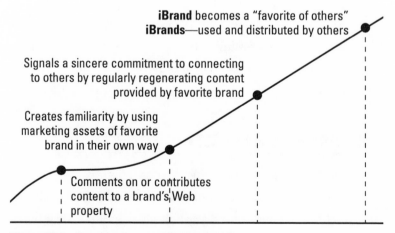

Figure 12.1   Process for establishing loyalty.

respond with more information that still may only be educational at this point. But you have begun introducing facets of your brand that this customer will find interesting and will connect to with a feeling of familiarity—"There's just something I like about this brand." Today, at the same time that this happening, the customer is building an **iBrand** of his or her own online.

For Chick-fil-A, this is the perfect time to talk about the role played by sign-toting cows in the company's brand persona. Their quirky humor and slightly offbeat attempts at communicating like humans are enjoyable. Over time, the bovine antics become familiar and synonymous with positive aspects of the brand's personality.

Successfully building relationships with customer **iBrands** depends on how well the company becomes a true friend of its customers. The key here is concern—about them as people, not profit centers. When you get down to it, it's about making and listening to likable, relevant conversation. (See Chapter 10: Conversation: What Matters Most for Marketers Now.) Growth always has been and always will be dependent on listening to and being heard by the customer. The only thing that has changed is how much more easily those conversations can happen today.

THE COST AND THE OPPORTUNITY

Many times the idea-killer that crosses the marketer's mind is, "We just don't have the time or the resources" to give each consumer **iBrand** the level of attention needed to truly raise the company's own brand equity. Well there's good news for those of little faith. Actually, we're talking about influencing only a relatively small number of people. The "friendships" with **iBrands** you want to develop are not as numerous as you might think. Even if you have a large, loyal online community following your brand, you may not have many at all who are actually dedicated consumer **iBrands**—relying on you to equip them with the raw materials for building their personal brand equity. Apply the 90-9-1 principle (www.90-9-1.com) and you'll see just how few true consumer **iBrand** relationships your brand likely has.

- **90** percent of users are the "audience," or lurkers. The people who tend to read or observe, but don't actively contribute.

    167,113 of Amazon's book reviews were contributed by just a few "top 100" reviewers.
- **9** percent of users are "editors," sometimes modifying content or adding to an existing thread, but rarely creating content from scratch.

    Over 50 percent of all the Wikipedia edits are done by just .7 percent of the users — 524 people.
- **1** percent of users are "creators," driving large amounts of the social group's activity. More often than not, these people are driving a vast percentage of the site's new content, threads, and activity.

    Just 0.16 percent of all visitors to YouTube upload videos to it, and 0.2 percent of visitors to Flickr upload photos.[2]

What a huge opportunity to reach out to the 90 percent and begin to bring some of them into the community in a deeper, more meaningful relationship. First you'll have to make a cyber connection with the individual: "I want to join this conversation because I like what this person knows, does, gets, and so on."

By equipping the 1 percent of **iBrands** with visible branding assets that bolster their **iBrand** equity, companies can leverage the vocal **iBrands** and let them begin to influence the 9 percent and 90 percent into wanting what the 1 percent has. This could be the beginning of the movement your brand has been yearning for but has been unable to articulate or create on its own.

MEASURE HOW WELL YOU INFLUENCE THE INFLUENTIALS

This new approach to marketing in a digital environment requires a new set of metrics to assess the value of building online **iBrand** equity. These metrics should include the existing customer's **iBrand**'s social networking map before a specific marketing initiative is undertaken. Then that should be compared to how it looks after the campaign. Is it expanding? By how much? Are more targeted prospects and enthusiastic customers moving into the company's marketsphere thanks to word-of-mouth networking? What's the impact on sales, transaction count, new orders, new leads, product movement, retail traffic, and so on?

It's all about the influence of the influentials. The greater an **iBrand**'s influence over her or his own marketsphere, defined as followers, friends, subscribers, and the like, the more equity she or he has as an **iBrand**. Today, consumers are looking for marketers who add value to that equity through unique opportunities to be heard, sharing relevant interests, and, most of all, providing something worth talking about—a special event, miracle app, better product, astonishing service, never-possible-before experience. Now marketers must adapt and augment their marketing models to consider the new opportunistic world of **iBrands**. It looks like we'll be living in a **Brand**-to-**iBrand** messaging future.

So what does this mean for the **iDirect** advertising agencies that now must provide interactive content expertise and build interactive, caring customer relationships online and offline that lead to profitable growth for a client's brand? Because brand managers must keep their primary focus on product design, service improvement, production process, and multichannel distribution, it's more important than ever to rely on the right advertising agency for vital **iDirect Marketing** and providing for the customer's **iBrand**. The agency of the future will be expert at adding value to the client's customer **iBrand** as well as the client's brand equity. It's interactive, creative teams will think about time frames that encompass the consumer **iBrand** life cycle. And they must develop programs that maximize how the client's entire enterprise contributes to the value and growth of its consumers' **iBrand** equity.

Notes

1. McGregor, Jena, "Customer Service Champs," *The 2008 Winners Special Report, BusinessWeek*, March 3, 2008, p. 47, 48.
2. McKee, Jake, "The 90-9-1 Principle," http://www.90-9-1.com/.

Chapter
13

The Keys to iDirect Marketing Success

Tim Suther

Senior Vice President,
Global Multichannel Marketing Services, Acxiom

Today's marketplace is a little like living next door to a train station. At first the roar is deafening. But as time goes by, the noise fades into the background. Soon it's ignored, just as if the noise is not there.

Consumers today are, in effect, living by the train station. They are bombarded every day with online and offline ads, pitches, offers, and deals. Increasingly, they are tuning most of it out. Research by Briggs and Stuart indicates that $112 *billion* a year is wasted on advertising that doesn't connect[1]—and new research shows that brands are overvalued by $4 *trillion*. Other research indicates that only 22 percent of Americans trust advertising compared to 45 percent who trust television talk shows.

The consumer is boss, and she has fired most of your advertising.

So how do you break through the noise online and offline to get your brand heard, trusted, and remembered? And how do you maximize results? The answer is in the new digitally enhanced **iDirect** and **iBranding** practices that will drive marketing supremacy in the future. Our research at Acxiom indicates that when you augment the conventional power of direct marketing and brand marketing with the intensely personal involvement now possible on the Web, you can earn an "order of magnitude" improvement for your return on marketing investment (ROMI) over the straightjacket of past practices.

Acxiom is a global interactive and direct marketing services firm. We retain data and insights on half a billion consumers around the globe, updated trillions of times a year. We've spent hundreds of millions of dollars over the last decade developing the technology to correlate consumer behavior with media spend so that our clients can capture better returns on their marketing investment. In this chapter you will discover how our experience, as the world's number one gatherer and analyzer of consumer data, supports the new **iDirect Marketing** paradigm. Based on recent experience serving many of the world's leading marketers, we believe that there are several fundamentals underlying the practice of **iDirect** that lead to significant increases in ROMI.

THE FIRST FUNDAMENTAL: DATA IS THE "NEW BLACK"

In a booming economy, it's easy to overlook the vital importance of data, the nerdy little sister to slick advertising. But in a financially down economy marketers speedily shifted to utilizing data to drive a better marketing return on investment. During the great recession of 2008–2009 belts tightened and the emphasis moved to making every dollar count. The result was a new focus on tracking and measurement of the marketing/ad spend.

What has often been missed is the rigorous discipline of correlating what is spent with the desired change in customer behavior. In tough times it becomes more important than ever to learn from every interaction. Data has become the "new black," the fashionable key to understanding why your customers behave the way they do. The analysis leading to that understanding enables you to more aggressively retain/grow and more rapidly acquire high-value new customers. The i in **iDirect** encompasses many

aspects of the new marketing, from interactive two-way communication to harvesting new sources of information and insights about prospects and customers. In today's economy nothing matters more than the meaningful information and real time view of Internet behavior that guides your ability to market directly with increased response and lower cost per sale.

The data you gather lays the groundwork for a booming ROMI. It empowers you to know the answer to such questions as:

- What media are your customers responding to and why?
- What message frequency offers the best performance?
- What are customers' explicit preferences and what have they *told* you they want?
- What does their behavior imply, and how does it help you determine what they *really* want?
- What are their differences in lifetime value, and how are they trending?
- How are your media investments performing in relation to your competition?

"Expanding your vision" by accumulating and analyzing relevant data is what drives breakthrough performance. Many firms maintain impressive data sets about their customers and all the interactions with visitors to the brand's Web site. But, unfortunately, the people attracted to your brand, at best, likely spend only 2 percent of their time in cyberspace with you. To put this in perspective, think about the busy lives your customers lead. Think of all the things they do on the Web: read the news, check e-mails, make social connections, get an up-to-the-minute weather report, compare prices and shop, watch videos, consult Wikipedia, and so on. Now how much time do you think they spend at your online properties? Insight into what they're doing with the 97, 98, or 99 percent of the time spent elsewhere can provide important growth opportunities for your business. And there is a vast array of syndicated, compiled, and industry data in existence just for that purpose.

Another critical dimension is the differentiated value of customers. Some of them buy more, cost less to service, and bring in added revenue by recommending you to their friends. These are your most valuable customers. If you fail to differentiate marketing spend by true customer value, you could miss a big chance to optimize business performance. In fact, our research indicates that if you simply concentrate marketing spend on customers most likely to rise to the top of the lifetime value ladder, you could see a three to five times higher "concentration multiplier."

Tracking and correlating marketing spend data to the resulting consumer behavior are the first fundamentals to keep in mind for successful **iDirect** marketing. Data—that nerdy little sister—is a knockout of a grown-up now. Make sure her insights are heard at the strategic planning table. Your bottom line—ROMI—will thank you for it.

THE SECOND FUNDAMENTAL: OPEN YOUR POCKETBOOK TO NEW COMMUNICATION CHANNELS

Many firms have invested heavily in systems to measure advertising and retail customer data. Unfortunately many of these readings remain channel- or product-specific. It's as if someone invested in a high-end home theater system and had a different tone coming out of each speaker. For marketers, this disharmony translates to underperformance and can lead to a counterproductive media spend. It takes an enterprising view of the customer to communicate in surround sound.

That's why another fundamental of **iDirect Marketing** is to be open-minded about securing a 360-degree view of consumer behavior across all of today's familiar, not so familiar, and entirely

unfamiliar channels. This principle extends the idea of correlating customer behavior to marketing spend *across all connection points*.

Remember that $112 billion of wasted advertising? Much of it is the result of programs being continued after they've lost their ability to deliver value in excess of their cost. Organizational dynamics within the agency/media axis often don't help. There is a powerful motivation for those owning specific capabilities or media to promote their own value. After all, jobs and profitable relationships are at stake. And, without an objective 360-degree view, any one option may sound reasonable. A multichannel perspective allows marketers to project an optimal program for each channel to root out the lowest-value initiatives and to calculate ROMI based on actual performance by channel.

Marketers and consumers alike face explosive growth in the number of shopping channels and media engagement options. For marketers, these options dramatically increase the challenge of getting today's media plan right. With the surge in online news media channels there not only is overlap but the effect of interrelated multiple buys as well. Consumers may be simultaneously using several modes of media and may be exposed to dozens or even hundreds of your messages before making a product choice. So which exposure gets the credit? A simplistic "last-ad-seen" model causes many firms to take away a distorted view of just which media placement contributed a share of the wasted $112 billion.

Finally, a 360-degree view enables progressive marketers simultaneously to optimize across four dimensions—segment, media, offer, and time. It also allows for full expression of the insights that only the i in **iDirect** can provide. You are now empowered to link your media investment to the differentiated value of targeted customers, retool media plans based on measured effectiveness by segment, identify the optimal balance between offer and response, and tune message frequency across channels. With a 360-degree view, you listen when the market talks.

THE THIRD FUNDAMENTAL: CONTENT CONFLUENCE

With consumers "living next to the train station," communications have to be relevant and engaging to drown out all the noise and produce a high-scoring outcome. Confluence fuses your insight about the consumer with the rest of what's needed in the marketing process. It connects the targeting to developing attention-grabbing creative and an enticing offer. To put it another way, confluence extends the ROMI from media buying to content creation.

Direct marketers have leveraged this principle for years. When direct mail is addressed to "occupant," it performs up to 15 times worse than a personalized, highly relevant piece.

With a well-constructed test matrix, direct marketers soon learn what the right message is and the right offer for the right person. Unfortunately, much of today's advertising outside of pinpointed

direct mail remains poorly targeted, and high-value customers often are exposed to the same creative as low-value customers.

Targeting the right customers misses a trick if it doesn't extend that insight into every aspect of the marketing continuum. Luckily, the technology of **iDirect** enables us to do this on the Web in a powerful and cost-effective way. The confluence of consumer insights, proven direct marketing know-how, and interactive digital media can make your communications more relevant and powerful than we ever thought possible.

EXECUTING IN A NEW COMFORT ZONE

The boost to reaching your advertising and marketing goals is found in the simultaneous application of the three fundamentals:

(1) data as the new black, (2) harmonizing media spend and a 360-degree customer view, and (3) the confluence of customer insights and content creation. These keys to optimizing performance will take you a long way toward success. But, far too often, you still can fall short if equal attention is not given to the art and science of proper execution.

Marketing executives often are frustrated by the gap between well-devised strategies and marketplace results. Research indicates that while most CMOs have confidence in a chosen strategy, only 30 percent believe in their firm's ability to execute it. It is interesting to note that 80 percent of CEOs think they offer a superior brand experience. Guess what? Only 8 percent of their customers agree with them.

In short, the old ways of execution have not kept pace with the new world of consumer expectations. It helps to understand how staying in their comfort zones have held companies back. History offers great lessons in "what could have been":

- Before the iPod, Sony dominated portable music.
- Before Google, Yellow Pages owned on-demand information.
- Before Netflix, Blockbuster controlled on-demand movie rentals.

All these firms had great customers, great products, and great people. They had insight into customers' needs and wants. They had deep relationships with distribution channels and supplier networks. In short, they had all the incumbent advantages. Yet none could withstand the success of their brilliant, strategic, and "executional" competitors. Upsetting traditional business models is often what wins.

It takes strategy *and execution* to survive the disruptive innovation of a fast-moving competitor. The first step is to assess whether "tried and true" is still true for your business. Will your competitive advantage stand up in the face of new technology and changing consumer preferences? The core function of an aligned organization with complementary processes, reliable metrics, and sound leadership is the ability to meet challenges with rapid and flawless execution of a valid strategic response.

The most difficult part of moving the company in a new direction is stepping out into the unknown. The challenge of moving out of a familiar comfort zone should never be underestimated. Entrenched interests, grounded in turf control and economic self-interest, can be formidable. As with any change, executing in a strange new comfort zone brings considerable anxiety at first, but it's an anxiety that success will diminish quickly. The real danger is in staying within a "tried-and-true" comfort zone that no longer is true.

DIRECT MARKETING IS NOW iDIRECT MARKETING

Early adopters have begun deploying **iDirect Marketing**, with eye-popping ROMI results. Not surprisingly, many of these firms have well-established direct marketing skills and assets. The success we are seeing among Acxiom's clients as they come to master what the i brings to **Direct** via the Internet is remarkable. Some examples include:

- A leading publisher increased digital conversions four-fold with a cohesive print and digital communication campaign. An innovative daily self-learning decision engine broke new ground.
- A leading hospitality firm was able to double its Web site revenue by integrating and analyzing outbound digital promotional data with a responder's digital footprint. Noting customer preferences on the Web site

enabled deep insights that drove future **iDirect** marketing success.

- A leading financial services firm saw a 17-fold increase in response rates by tailoring information provided based on household viewer profiles. Technology available now on millions of U.S. cable set-top boxes enables viewers to request information via their handheld remote control in response to television commercials. Applying direct marketing principles to interactive TV can drive spectacular results.

- A leading technology company identified common product questions and incorporated them into a multi-channel life-cycle marketing program. The result? More than $2 million per year saved in call center cost displacement, $2.5 million per year in reduced marketing expenses, and more than $200 million generated in annual revenue.

- A leading retailer saw more than a seven-fold improvement in Web spend by combining digital and mobile promotional efforts. Mobile buyers, in particular, are a lucrative segment, with an average income 23 percent higher than an Internet-only buyer segment. Mobile buyers also spend more than double what an Internet-only buyer spends. As this leading retailer can attest, reaching affluent buyers through mobile is not a strategy for tomorrow. It's here to be used today (Learn more from Michael Becker in Chapter 7.)

- A leading advertiser realized over four times the revenue per ad dollar by leveraging the "concentration multiplier." Instead of displaying messages equally to all Web site visitors without regard to their potential value, the advertiser targeted only those likely to become top-percentile customers. Making the selection may involve a modest increase in media spend, but the resulting, directly measured revenue produced dramatic increases over time.

MARKETING PYRITE

In the nineteenth century, gold prospectors were often fooled by pyrite, or "fools gold." Unfortunately, marketing pyrite similarly often leads marketing prospectors to make bad decisions. These miscalculations are caused by the "foolers" waiting out there to upset your best laid **iDirect Marketing** plans. Here are a few examples:

- *Measurement systems that imply that all customers have equal value.* While no advertiser really believes that all customers are equal, evaluating campaigns solely by response rate, click-through, or even conversion rates can encourage marketers to downplay relative lifetime value in favor of large numbers of responses. Many offerings require time to break even, so converting a buyer who is likely to leave quickly is a bad business decision. Acquiring customers who don't cross-buy or repeat-buy or have high servicing costs also is likely to earn a subpar or negative return.

- *Measurement systems that give the last ad all the credit.* The effects of media are interrelated and overlapping. Nevertheless, digital marketers regularly give full credit to the last ad seen (often a search query). This greatly overestimates the influence of the last ad. Don't agree? Try lowering your demand-generating marketing spend (i.e., television, e-mail, display, etc.), and watch your search volume decline. Search fulfills, but does not generate, demand. Many marketers would benefit from moving some paid search volume into true demand-generating programs and organic search (72 percent of Google's click-throughs are from organic links).

- *Measurement systems that focus solely on cost per impression.* With inexpensive media widely available, it is tempting to forgo targeting and blast away. Do so at your own peril. For example, a highly targeted e-mail will perform 15 times as well as a broadcast message. Consumers have shown they will ignore (or worse) irrelevant communications. So, while impressions may be cheap, recapturing a lost customer is expensive. Create a value per thousand metric to complement traditional cost per thousand calculations.

- *Because you can, you should.* Today's depth and breadth of acquiring consumer insight creates both opportunity and danger. The consumer is sensitive to both overstimulation and perceptions of privacy intrusion. Privacy regulations are stringent and vary from country to country. It is imperative to know what the rules are and to practice restraint to avoid costly violations and/or lose your customers' trust. At Acxiom we were one of the first to create a chief privacy officer position more than 20 years ago. It was one of the smartest and most appreciated decisions we ever made. Last year alone, we helped our clients avoid 3 billion privacy violations.

- *Executive sponsorship.* Firms can champion their confidence in the power of **iDirect Marketing** by appointing a chief **iDirect** officer (CiDO). The CiDO would provide knowledge of the latest examples of **iDirect** innovation. The CiDO would bring invaluable expertise to the early planning stages and make certain the "data people" and the "interactives" get an opportunity to contribute their insights in shaping brand strategy at the highest level.

WHERE DO YOU GO FROM HERE?

As we have seen, the customary tried-and-true marketing maxims left over from another era generate subpar ROMI, declining brand value, and dangerously low levels of consumer trust. The fundamentals of **iDirect Marketing** are increasingly seen as today's lowest cost and most effective means of elevating ROMI.

To achieve the full potential of the confluence of digital and direct, nothing is more important than the accumulation and analysis of insightful behavioral data. Is your measurement of which customers are most valuable reliable? How reliable? Do you know what form of communication is most likely to influence decisions those customers make? Are you certain that prior knowledge of differentiated payoff is driving a differentiated investment? Now that every marketer is an **iDirect**, are you keeping pace with the most up-to-date direct response acquisition and retention techniques of the digital era?

A full-scale customer view helps reduce data blind spots—those costly lapses in information that can cause overinvestment in weak channels at the expense of the best.

How about hanging a sign on a wall in the conference area used for planning that proclaims: "It's the data, stupid."

By unleashing behavioral information that shapes ideal one-to-one communication, the new marketing accomplishes so much more for so much less than yesterday's mass media bombardment of the consumer ever did. The right form of customer engagement generates the right data that drives the right promotions that realize the right outcome every time you go to market.

Executing **iDirect** initiatives when it requires going outside your familiar comfort zone may be the greatest challenge ahead. Doing things differently requires no additional cost, no new personnel, and no new hardware. But it does require an organization's willingness to embrace change. To quote General Eric Shinseki, Secretary of Veterans Affairs, "If you dislike change, you're going to dislike irrelevance even more." An extraordinary rate of change is the reality of our time. The irrelevance it can cause is the greatest threat you face today.

Embrace the new, pacesetting **iDirect** and **iBranding** ideas presented in the wide-ranging chapters of this book. Move boldly into the new future of marketing directly. Leave your competition at the starting gate while you race ahead.

Note

1. Briggs, R. and G. Stuart, *What Sticks* (Chicago: Kaplan 2006).

Appendix

iDirect's Secret Weapon: The New Testing Mandate

Jose Cebrian

Group Director, Acxiom Global
Multichannel Marketing Services

Ben Rothfeld

Director of Marketing Strategy, Acxiom Global
Multichannel Marketing Services

YOUR ADVERTISING DOES NOT WORK

Maybe you got a 5 percent response rate to your e-mail. Maybe
your ad contributed to a 25 percent unaided awareness score. But
those figures mean that 95 percent didn't respond to the e-mail or
that 75 percent of the target ad audience for your brand doesn't
know who you are.

More accurately, your advertising may work for some of those you want to reach, but it doesn't work for many, many more of them. While no advertising will ever reach 100 percent effectiveness, far too many marketers fail to build upon what they have achieved to drive even greater success.

There is a long-established practice for doing better than what you now believe is your best. It is called testing. This appendix to "Reinventing Interactive and Direct Marketing" raises the testing battle cry of the new **iDirect Marketing** paradigm. As the content of the preceding chapters came together, it became apparent that "test, test, test" was a subtheme running through the entire book. It also became apparent that a discussion of the state of the art of testing today would be of great value to would-be **iDirect** marketers. As completion date for the originally planned manuscript approached, the decision was made to cover this vital subject in this appendix to the book's content.

With the arrival of the Web, it has never been easier or more affordable to improve every aspect of your communications. If you are not taking full advantage of the new possibilities for improving results dramatically, at least you have lots of company. To cite just one example, fewer than half of all Internet retailers test e-mail subject lines, by far the easiest attribute to test and a component that can make an enormous difference in the outcome from any e-mail.*

Bringing up the need for testing often elicits groans and the rolling of eyes from marketers. Resistance comes not only from the creative types who disdain cold logic but also from the account people who need to justify the additional time and resources testing requires. However, the right attitude about testing not only improves every marketing effort it touches, but it also makes real the promise of making one-to-one marketing pay off in a big way.

* Internet Retailer, "E-Mail Marketing" survey conducted by Knowledge Marketing, October 2008, and quoted in *eMarketer* on November 26, 2008.

Traditionally, testing meant exposing a sample of an audience to a different version of an offer or creative and measuring results. While today's testing retains that essence, it now partners with digital technology and analytics to drive results not only at the whole audience level and not only at the segment level but at the individual level.

Simply put, testing is learning. Marketers who do not test do not learn. Learning makes marketing communications smarter, both immediately and over time. Now, in today's digital **iDirect** environment, the power to take test results to unprecedented heights becomes magnified a hundredfold.

TESTING AS LEARNING

Where your initial efforts end, testing begins. Look at it this way: when a marketer finds that his prospects or customers respond better to an e-mail with a large product picture than one with a small product picture, he learns how the communication display pictures matter to the consumer. While in and of itself, this mere fact has little impact on the brand as a whole, it becomes a building block in customer knowledge. In the aggregate, understanding many of these building blocks helps the marketer understand her audience in more meaningful ways. For instance, knowing that customers not only respond best to larger pictures and also like short copy and user testimonials might suggest that other marketing materials—not just e-mail—would benefit from a highly visual approach backed by real-life examples.

The Internet channel has supercharged the traditional test-and-learn process. We have yet to exit the early stages of discovering what we can do to speed up the learning process and to convert that newfound knowledge to newfound improvement in the bottom line. Because now marketers track individual responses more easily than ever before, they speedily develop detailed statistical portraits of their customers and prospects. By using database management tools well within the reach of most organizations, marketers can amass customer data online by recognizing consumers via e-mail addresses and cookies. E-mail addresses help recognize the customer when he clicks from an e-mail to a landing page or when she logs in at a brand's Web site. As a result, most marketers pay particular attention to the accumulation of opt-in e-mail addresses. Cookies similarly recognize customers on the brand site and via advertising networks where customers opt in and are identified at the segment or household level. Activities conducted by the customers who have these e-mail addresses and cookies then become attributes of the customers' file. Assuming that all these inputs end up properly reflected in the customer database, the marketer gets a broad view of customer behavior. While this kind of data integration requires substantial expertise, our company's own experience suggests that by working with the right partners, any marketer, large or small, can achieve this singular view of the customer in the near term.

You now can learn much faster than ever before what an individual customer responds to across multiple channels such as e-mail, search, and display (banner advertising) as well as on the brand's Web site. These inputs, when collated in a composite view and combined with information from a legacy database that the marketer may have, leads to smart decisions about how and when to market to each segment.

Continually, testing offers in both e-mail and display advertising enables a marketer to adjust the offer for the best channel. Or, by analyzing response patterns, the marketer can understand whether the customer prefers one specific channel over another. Cutting-edge marketers combine these data points into information from call centers, point-of-sale (POS) systems, and even hand-held device–equipped sales associates.

Marketers can also use a technique called *link categorization* to get additional details on responses. With link categorization, an organization adds a consistent set of identifiers to links, such as product categories (A = apparel, B = beauty, C = consumables). For testing purposes, marketers can rotate the categories of links in a communication to see what most interests the target audience. Customers who click consistently on, say, apparel links will begin to see more apparel offers in their communications.

For one of our clients, we tracked what form of offer its customers clicked on in e-mails and then populated more of those types of offers into future e-mails. Conversions doubled because the company learned what individual customers wanted and then provided more of what they wanted.

Naturally, the outpouring of data in a digital era calls for many skills that go well beyond basic A/B testing. With so much to deal with, skilled data analytics now moves to the center of the stage. We take a look at this emerging new focus on analytics farther along in this appendix.

TESTING AND HOW IT GOT THAT WAY

A little history sheds light on how classic direct marketers used testing in the twentieth century. They merely wanted to find the best possible execution for a specific piece of direct mail or direct response advertising. Successful control pieces ran for decades. Most famously, in 1975, the *Wall Street Journal* debuted a direct mail solicitation that began:

> On a beautiful late spring afternoon, twenty-five years ago, two young men graduated from the same college. They were very much alike, these two young men. Both had been better than average students, both were personable and both — as young college graduates are — were filled with ambitious dreams for the future.
>
> Recently, these men returned to their college for their 25th reunion.

They were very much alike. Both were happily married. Both had three children. And both, it turned out, had gone to work for the same Midwestern manufacturing company, and were still there.

But there was a difference. One of the men was manager of a small department of that company. The other was its president.

The letter ran largely unchanged until 2003 — 31 years* Untold numbers of that letter's recipients came to the conclusion that they would have a better chance of ending up like the company president if they subscribed to the *Journal*. Just think how reassuring the prospering *Wall Street Journal* found it to know that its advertising best practices were indeed the best.

As direct mailers became direct marketers across an increasing number of communication channels, their strategies and their testing became more sophisticated as well. They tested not at the total audience level, but at the segment level. Testing at the segment level allowed an even greater degree of precision, with creative and offer marketing targeted to increasingly smaller groups of like-minded people. The ultimate goal — never reached — was one-to-one marketing.

Simple A/B (test-and-control) tactics gave way to complex multivariate tactics. Multivariate tactics allowed marketers to test more variables at once. In a single campaign, given large enough sample cells, you could test long copy versus short copy, dollars-off offer versus gift-with-purchase offer, illustration versus photo versus no graphic, and small-type headline versus large-type headline. This approach not only allowed brands to create a high-powered version faster, but it also allowed them to understand the overall impact of a specific attribute more clearly.

---

* *Internet Marketing Newswatch*, December 28, 2006, http://www
.imnewswatch.com/archives/2006/12/martin_conroy_d.html?visitFrom=2.

Table A.1 is a matrix that indicates the click-to-open ratio for an e-mail test that we conducted for a hotel chain. Click-to-open (CTO) measures the percentage of people who clicked on an offer in an e-mail compared to the total number of people who opened the e-mail, thus indicating the strength of the content and offers irrespective of open rates. Half of the audience got an offer for a London hotel, and the other half got an offer for a Paris hotel. In addition, half of each group got an e-mail with no photo, and half got an e-mail with a photo.

Table A.1   Click-to-open (CTO) ratio for Different Versions of a Hotel Promotional e-mail

	London	**Paris**
No photo	8.73%	6.68%
Photo	8.06%	7.49%

The hotel marketer learned that overall, the no-photo e-mail for London performed best. But it also learned that overall, offers for London performed better than did offers for Paris. Incidentally, the test also suggests that pictures help sell a hotel in Paris but not London.

As a simple two-by-two (or four-cell) matrix, this test represents the simplest possible multivariate test. Experienced direct marketers can, with effort, conduct substantially more involved tests with a dozen or more variables. Even a novice tester could see that as tests include more variables and more segments, it becomes increasingly more difficult for humans to eyeball results and make decisions. Thus **iDirect** marketers must turn to analytics—the link between testing and the marketing automation of the future—to evolve from testing into marketing automation.

THE RISE OF ANALYTICS

Analytics, of course, predated marketing via the Web. Direct marketers have used analytics for years to target the right customers and prospects for a specific offer or mailing. But consider what analytics does; it involves using mathematical models based on data such as product ownership or demographics to predict how individuals will respond to a particular offer. To put it another way, analytics determines the best offer for a particular individual. While many marketers would discern a bright line between testing and analytics, it makes sense to view analytics as an evolution of testing. After all, analytics of this nature depends on learning—the learning generated by testing.

The analytics model learns based on whatever data the analysts feed into it—e-mail response, zip code, purchase history, and what have you. Unlike traditional testing, analytics essentially tests before the fact. The model uses correlative analysis to find patterns not necessarily visible to human analysts. It can find, for instance, that the best indicator of product preference may be a customer's age or family size or some combination of those two data points. Most famously, Amazon.com does this every time a visitor returns to the site with its recommendations ("people who bought X also liked Y"). In that case, Amazon selects the product to recommend based on how the visitor's purchase history compares with the purchase histories of every other Amazon customer. Netflix compares renters' requests among one another to find the films that complement what customers ask for. Netflix, in fact, so firmly grasps the importance of this kind of analytics that it has offered a $1 million prize to anyone who can develop a better model for predicting what movies a customer would want. As of this writing, the field of competitors for this prize has narrowed to two. The winner must beat the current model by at least 10 percent, but what if it beats the model by 20 percent, 30 percent, or more? Imagine the payback on that $1 million spent to find a new system to test.

Getting back to **iDirect Marketing**, the analytics approach has created such tools as the next logical product model. Based on the history of an individual's purchases, a retailer can make an increasingly accurate guess as to the next offer to make to him or her.

For one computer hardware manufacturer, our company realized a 20 percent jump in revenues by employing a next logical product model in a series of e-commerce e-mails.

Analytics of this nature works hand in hand with testing. More data, created by conversions or nonconversions of offers spit out by a next-logical product model, help sharpen the accuracy of the model. In the case of the hardware manufacturer above, the e-mails alternate between those with static offers (everyone sees the same set) and those with decision engine-driven e-mails to prevent offer burnout. By constantly introducing new offers, the approach ensures that customers do not keep seeing the same offers over and over again. These static offers, in fact, help test the model and drive it toward more appealing offers.

Analytics, then, points the way toward greater personalization. The combination of frequent testing and advanced analysis can help answer age-old marketing questions such as:

- What offers will most appeal to a customer?
- How often should a marketer contact a customer and in which channel(s)?
- What kind of copy, images, and overall design appeal to a customer?

All that marketers need do is apply the right kind of testing and follow up with precise application of analytics. With the **iDirect** mindset, the marketer must always push the envelope on testing and analytics because of a fundamental belief in the power of admitting, "Maybe I don't know."

SO WHY DOESN'T EVERYONE DO THIS NOW?

Naturally, this advanced approach to testing isn't easy, or all marketers would be doing it. Several key barriers—not one of them immovable in and of itself—separate marketers from reaping the rewards of **iDirect** testing.

Cost always rises to the top in any discussion of testing. Traditional direct mailers may find the cost issue puzzling. After all, testing in direct mail requires multiple print runs of expensive mailing packages, whereas online communications scale at essentially no cost. However, simply testing two different versions of an e-mail does require doubling the creative resources necessary. In the context of direct mail, a single extra creative execution seems minor in comparison to overall printing and mailing costs for the campaign. But in the online world, the cost of second execution may exceed the total sending costs of a campaign. Smart marketers know that testing will reap rewards, but those rewards may take a few iterations to come about. And many marketers lack the organizational freedom to prove ideas over time. A big problem is the mistaken view of the cost of testing. Rather than being seen as an extra or disproportionate expense in a low-cost digital advertising campaign, it must be viewed as an investment in the long-term growth of the business. Only when viewed in that way will there be investment in multiple testing on a sufficient scale to see improvements of 100 percent, 200 percent, or more in ROI.

Part of the trouble arises from the types of clients who depend on e-communications compared with those who traditionally favored direct mail. Financial services companies invested in direct mail because of the relative sizes of customer lifetime values. Successful mailings for credit cards or insurance policies easily paid for themselves and the costs of optimization. While financial services marketers also take advantage of online communications, others have joined them, notably retailers. With the narrow profit margins across the board in retail, those marketers have shown greater reluctance to invest in testing that does not produce immediate results. Still, in our own tests with retailers, we've seen profitable gains with simple tests, and the ones who test the most gain the most.

Some traditional testers reject extensive testing because of a perceived inability to isolate the results coming from where the test is taking place. With TV, outdoor, direct mail, e-mail, search engine marketing, and display all going on at the same time, a marketer cannot fully control all other influences on a given channel. Even if the marketer prevents a sample from seeing all online materials, he or she cannot prevent those consumers from seeing mass media communications.

We know a national marketer who sends an e-mail to a subscriber only once every 90 days to ensure that the marketer can isolate that campaign activity. We agree that marketers should not overmail, but we think that this particular marketer should get significantly more aggressive—at least once a month, if not once per week excluding transactional messages. But it's seen as a customer service issue. Well, it's a customer service issue that costs shareholders money! We take the approach that marketing must go on and that we make do with what we have. Take results as directional information until full analysis counters the point.

Legacy technology often forms a barrier to smart testing and analytics. Many marketers keep customer information on one database, e-mail response on another, targeting information on another, and transactional behavior on yet another. In turn, these marketers lack a Rosetta Stone to help these databases talk to one another. While we have yet to find an insurmountable technology issue, we recognize that getting databases to talk with one another involves a cost, a factor discussed above. But making the technology work together also requires marketers to reach out and work with other entities in an organization whose goals do not necessarily align with theirs.

As with almost everything in the corporate world, turf matters. Marketers must overcome political battles to make a test successful for the company as a whole. Depending on the business, a brand's homepage may represent some of the most important real estate a marketer owns. Way too often, we see divisional allotments of homepage space or even mandates that a specific banner will dominate the homepage to appease one party or another. That's just not smart.

We perform a lot of Web personalization testing. Web personalization fine-tunes the Web site to drive conversions based on simple A/B splits of content or more robust testing of splits based on segments of customers—for example, those who search for the term "car" versus those who come from the southwest versus those who are repeat visitors from the southeast. At the end of the day, we argue that the homepage demands testing the most because visitors have acted on your calls to action in search, outdoor, e-mail, and so on. Now they have visited the Web site with intent, and the conversion path requires optimization.

But very often, the people who own search or e-mail do not own the Web site. So setting up a test often requires the involvement of information technology (IT), at least in the beginning. Then, to complicate the issue more, marketing must fight more turf battles over real estate on other key pages. Only the adoption of **iDirect** at the highest corporate levels will minimize these turf battles.

Take, for example, one travel company that we worked with. It had invested in learning what combination of placement and messaging would drive the greatest yield in terms of reservations, which was great. We helped the company design the test and then developed the creative. Great so far, but it lost a turf battle over what it could remove or change on the landing page. This marketer had to settle for much less bold testing than the situation demanded. Unsurprisingly, the test results showed no key difference in results because the changes to the landing page were so small and meaningless that they essentially had no effect. And together we wasted time. The test is back on track, and we are working on making major changes to the landing page so we can get measurable results.

Lastly, new ideas introduced in testing may require the cooperation of the marketer's legal team. Need we say more?

WHY IT'S WORTH IT: HOW TO THINK ABOUT TESTING TODAY

So what is testing today? In so many ways, the testing of today resembles the testing of the past. Then as now, marketers want to increase yield, in whatever way they may define it—online purchase, event registrations, site traffic, brand awareness, and the like. And marketers still test many of the same things—segmentation, creative, copy, offers. Similar to how the great cars of yesteryear got people from A to B but pale in comparison to modern autos, yesterday's tests do not compare with what marketers can achieve today. Testing today is faster, far more multivariate, more political, and more tuned in to analytics. Yet for most marketers it is underutilized.

Depending on the size of an e-mail list or number of visits to a particular page, a marketer can complete a full test and roll out the winning combinations all within a few hours. This speed drives great excitement but does not always drive significant results. The dependence on speed often compels marketers to test the things more easily under their control. Compare this attitude with the old joke about someone looking for his wallet under a streetlight not because that's where he dropped it but because it's where the light is. Many marketers prefer testing simple swaps like short copy versus long copy even though testing offers might drive greater results simply because they can rewrite copy more easily than they can develop new offers. Perhaps the greatest oversight lies in not testing the current positioning strategy against a totally new presentation of the proposition.

Marketers should not waste time on tests that provide little value, such as day of week tests or time of day tests. E-mailers often ask,

"When should we send our e-mails?" A few years ago, an e-mail service provider began publishing figures on the best day of the week to send e-mail. One study showed that e-mails launched on Wednesdays enjoyed the highest open and click rates. Guess what happened? Lots of marketers read that report and began mailing on Wednesdays. The following quarter, the same e-mail service provider found that Thursdays worked best. Rinse, lather, repeat.

While our own tests for clients have shown little reward for these efforts, it doesn't mean that it won't work in some cases. The point is that these are tweaks to a well-optimized program; marketers will not find bang for the buck here. But marketers do gravitate toward them because they can control them without any major input or push-back from other groups, both internal and external. Learn quickly which attributes matter to the brand and test those as often as possible. Figure A.1 summarizes our company's experience with the importance of specific attributes:

Figure A.1   Modifying different aspects of communications campaigns can have drastically different effects in response.

iDirect testing involves trying to increase yield within dependable channels such as e-mail and search while at the same time testing new media forms against each other to see what works and to get a head start on building a corporate competency in that new technology.

iDirect testing means optimizing the entire conversion path, from the start of the selling process to check out (and beyond) to drive the most profitable conversions and increase customer lifetime value.

iDirect testing means harnessing analytics to testing to drive new thinking and new approaches. In today's marketing world we must test new technologies against what we currently rely upon to see if the new technology pays off at that moment in time. As online budgets continue to grow, the key question is where to spend the next dollar best. In some cases, a marketer has maxed out spending on something that works extremely well, as with certain keyword buys. Even in going this route, companies face built-in limitations. If it is a low-volume word, then a marketer cannot allocate millions of dollars to it because it cannot be spent.

Examples of new technologies that marketers have tested into over the last couple of years include testing behaviorally targeted display (banners targeted based on the user's previous browsing) against contextual display (banners targeted based on what's on the page). Today, leading marketers allocate money to test online videos and even video in e-mail. So you must gather up the courage to apportion some of your budget to try new things to see if they have a chance of working out for your company. If they do work, then your company will invest in marketing that way or hire a vendor who has that competency. The key driver is to always put enough money behind something to actually get a measurable result.

iDirect testing requires a good bit of project management and some political savvy. Today the marketer often must coordinate with multiple parties to accomplish real results breakthroughs. You may need help to develop a test plan, to coordinate that test plan among vendors and agencies, to make sure that the technology is set up correctly, to work internally and with a vendor to make sure the data flow allows for thorough analysis, and then to work internally to get legal approval on the offers and creative. And you will need to acquire the resources to get landing pages created and customized. All in all, no small order.

The secret of full-scale **iDirect** testing lies in utilizing vendors to take the burden off your IT staff. Your experience may parallel where we were in the early days of the digital era, when we first learned about some of the tools available to us. We developed test plans that resembled Russian novels—long, dense, and complicated. After running into objections from both our own and our clients' IT departments, we learned how to reduce the number of tests and the complexities to produce testing matrixes we could execute more consistently and cost-effectively.

Lastly, **iDirect** testing means working with analytics to ensure that communications work not just in the aggregate but also on the individual level. Even the most efficient testing methods can cover only so many variables at one time; more than a dozen really start to strain current processes. The challenge for **iDirect** marketers lies in getting beyond that limitation.

Employing advanced analytics allows marketers to narrow down the possibilities to the most likely combination of attributes that serve as a great first step for constructing a realistic testing program.

Together, testing and analytics will not only improve your marketing, but it will constantly improve it. When it comes to testing, take the Japanese concept of *kaizen*, or constant improvement, to heart. *Kaizen* can help improve marketing communications through testing the way the Japanese improved their car production through constantly improving every aspect of the manufacturing process.

With each new wave of digital technology, you can look forward to greater optimization of response and a decreasing amount of effort to bring it about. After the initial planning and development stages, the algorithm does the heavy lifting. While today's capabilities do not yet reach the level of marketing automation — a 100 percent hands-off process — a lot less human oversight is required than in testing plans of old.

Smart marketers have always understood the power of testing. **iDirect** marketers are seizing upon the new technologies and techniques of the digital era to turn testing into a secret weapon that can lead to a phenomenal competitive advantage when fully employed in today's tough business environment.

Index

Meet the Authors

About Michael Becker

Michael Becker, a groundbreaking leader in mobile marketing, is vice president of mobile strategies for iLoop Mobile, one of America's leading mobile marketing solutions providers. Becker is the global and North American vice chairperson for the Mobile Marketing Association and a founding member of the Direct Marketing Association's mobile council. He is coauthor of *Web Marketing All-in-One for Dummies*, contributing author to *Mobile Internet for Dummies*, and coeditor of the *International Journal of Mobile Marketing*. Recently he was awarded the prestigious Direct Marketing Education Foundation 2009 Rising Stars Award.

About Michael Caccavale

Michael Caccavale is CEO of Pluris Marketing and holds an MBA from Babson College and a Bachelor of Science degree in engineering from Rensselaer Polytechnic Institute. His 20 years of marketing expertise in the retail, financial services, telecommunications, media, and health-care industries have deeply involved him in marketing technology development, strategic analysis, marketing process improvement, and advanced analytical optimization techniques. Caccavale also has specialized experience in media management across multiple points of consumer online and offline engagement. Prior to joining Pluris, Caccavale spent time at Procter & Gamble and founded Aperio, a leading marketing services firm.

About Richard Cross

Richard Cross is president of Cross World Network, a marketing consultancy (rcross@crossworldnetwork.com) he founded in 1987, and he is coauther of *Customer Bonding: Pathway to Lasting Customer Loyalty*. Cross's career spans 35 years of marketing innovation and thought leadership including 15 years with *Consumer Reports* magazine where he increased circulation to over 5 million readers. He has served as contributing editor to *Direct Marketing* magazine and both founded and served as editor-in-chief of *Case-in-Point*, a bimonthly publication focusing on building and utilizing customer databases. Currently he works with his clients to integrate traditional marketing practices with new Internet-based digital technologies.

About Lucas Donat

Lucas Donat is executive creative director and founding partner of Donat/Wald, located in Santa Monica, California. The ad agency has generated over $1 billion in sales for clients that include eHarmony, Hotwire, Movielink, SouthBeachDiet.com, LegalZoom, Mattel Toys, 1 800 Dentist, and ServiceMaster. Donat has directed and produced scores of DRTV television commercials throughout his career. He was the primary architect behind the advertising success of eHarmony.com, and is credited with making the brand a household name. eHarmony is now responsible for an average of 236 marriages a day, about 2 percent of all U.S. marriages annually.

About John A. Greco, Jr.

John A. Greco, Jr., president and chief executive officer of the Direct Marketing Association (DMA), had a 19-year career at AT&T that included a broad range of marketing and business development positions as well as five years as director of AT&T's Consumer Laboratory Center of Excellence at AT&T Bell Laboratories. In 1996, Greco moved to R. R. Donnelley & Sons as senior vice president of marketing and technology, later becoming senior vice president of marketing and business development. In 2000 he became president and CEO of the Yellow Pages Integrated Media Association, and in 2004 he was named CEO of the Direct Marketing Association.

About David M. Hughes

David M. Hughes is CEO of The Search Agency, with hands-on management of its product, technology, operations, and sales. Prior to The Search Agency, Hughes served as senior vice president of corporate development for United Online, where he developed new products to be offered to NetZero/Juno customers. He is an industry leader in developing and implementing search services, broadband services, and strategic relationships. Prior to United Online, he was a management consultant with the Boston Consulting Group and an associate with Mercer Management Consulting. Hughes is a graduate of Harvard University's Graduate School of Business Administration and was awarded the Dean's Award for leadership.

About Joseph Jaffe

As crayon's founder, president, and chief interruptor, Joseph Jaffe is one of the most sought-after digital era consultants, speakers, and thought leaders. His vision for the future of marketing lies behind many of crayon's proprietary approaches, and it infuses the company's work for clients such as Panasonic, Kraft, American Airlines, and Facebook. Jaffe is the creator of the popular Jaffe Juice blog and podcast, the star of the JaffeJuice TV Web video show, and the author of two groundbreaking books: *Join the Conversation* and *Life after the 30-Second Spot*. His third book, *Flip the Funnel*, will be published in early 2010.

About Michael McCathren

Michael McCathren is a 25-year restaurant executive whose experience includes operations, finance, and marketing responsibilities at leading casual and fast-food marketers. He joined Chick-fil-A in 2004 and today serves as its newly proclaimed conversation catalyst. McCathren crafted the company's digital marketing strategy and dramatically increased the brand's presence online with branded Web sites for franchisees, an enhanced e-mail strategy, and a unique relationship with customers on Facebook. Recent speaking engagements include Advertising Week, 1 to 1 Media, "Chick-fil-A: Fast Food Dishes Five Star Service," and the American Marketing Association's "Sharing Your Brand in the Social Space."

About Jeanniey Mullen

Jeanniey Mullen is the chief marketing officer for Zinio and for VIVmag. She has global responsibilities for the growth of America's leading digital magazine distributor. Prior to Zinio, Mullen was a senior partner and global executive director at OgilvyOne Worldwide. She founded the E-Mail Experience Council, ran her own advertising agency, and played a leading role in the development of e-mail marketing inside advertising agencies in the late 1990s at Grey Direct. She is the coauthor of the recently published *Email Marketing; An Hour a Day*, and a frequent featured speaker at e-mail, interactive, and digital marketing events.

About Melissa Read, Ph.D.

Melissa Read, Ph.D., is vice president of research and innovation for Engauge. Dr. Read leverages psychological insights to explain, predict, and influence online behavior. She enables marketers to deepen customer relationships and drive profitable revenue growth. At Engauge, Dr. Read spearheads the agency's digital strategic thinking. She earned her doctorate in psychology and is a former college professor. She frequently speaks on the psychology of marketing at national conferences and contributes to industry publications. Her research has been published in *Psychological Science* and has been presented at Harvard and the Beckman Institute for Advanced Science and Technology.

About Janet Rubio

Janet Rubio is adept at combining business acumen with a genuine delight in working with bright people. She led Dell's direct marketing efforts when the company expanded from a $750 million to a $2 billion valuation. In 1995, she formed Direct Impact, shaping the agency into a nationally recognized leader in advanced data analytics and direct marketing innovation. In 2007, Halyard Capital acquired Direct Impact as the initial building block of what would become the Engauge enterprise, a new marketing solutions agency model. Her current pioneering executive management role at Engauge is serving as the agency's first chief insights officer.

About Don E. Schultz

Don E. Schultz is professor (emeritus-in-service) of integrated marketing communications at Northwestern University in Evanston, Illinois. He holds a BBA from the University of Oklahoma and an MA and Ph.D. from Michigan State University. He is president of Agora, Inc., a global marketing, communication, and branding consulting firm. Professor Schultz lectures, conducts seminars, delivers conference keynotes, and consults for blue-chip marketers on five continents. He is the author/coauthor of more than 18 books, over 100 trade, academic, and professional articles, and is the editor of the *International Journal of Integrated Marketing Communication*.

About Tim Suther

Tim Suther is Acxiom senior vice president Global Multichannel Marketing Services. An officer of Acxiom, he leads the company's businesses covering digital media, agency services, and technology, as well as the marketing of database services and products. In this role, he directs Acxiom's global efforts. Suther has been with Acxiom since 2005 and is renowned for his 26 years of experience in applying technology-enabled business models to achieve transformational results in a variety of industries. Suther has served as senior vice president and general manager at Metavante, the financial services technology firm, and president at Protagona Worldwide, the publicly traded marketing software firm.

About Greg Verdino

Greg Verdino is chief strategy officer at the marketing consultancy, crayon, which focuses on marketing innovation, social media, new technologies, and emerging channels. Verdino writes one of the Web's most influential marketing blogs (www.gregverdino.com), is a go-to social media expert for business media reporters, and is a frequent conference speaker. He is completing his first book, *microMARKETING*, slated for a mid-2010 release from McGraw-Hill. Prior to crayon, Greg was vice president of emerging channels at Digitas and held senior positions in noted marketing companies including Akamai, Arbitron, Blau Marketing Technologies, Saatchi & Saatchi, and Wunderman.

About Engauge

Engauge is proud to sponsor the publication of *Reinventing Interactive and Direct Marketing*, edited and inspired by our Chairman, Stan Rapp. It is a book that dares to address what must change in marketing fundamentals for the new digital era. As a pioneer in the practice of **iDirect Marketing** and **iBranding**, Engauge connects data-driven insights with innovative creative online and offline to fuel growth for our clients. Our focus on measuring performance is reflected in our name, Engauge, and we serve a rapidly growing list of some of America's blue-chip marketers. You can learn more about us at www.engauge.com.

About Stan Rapp

Business Builder

Stan Rapp is a marketing icon who has twice served as Chairman/CEO of global advertising agencies with combined annual revenues that now add up to over a billion dollars. As cofounder of Rapp Collins (rebranded as RAPP), he spent 23 years at the helm of what grew to become one of the top five U.S. advertising agencies. While he was CEO of McCann Relationship Marketing (MRM) and while he served for six years on the Board of McCann Erickson WorldGroup, MRM revenue increased seven-fold. In his current endeavor as Chairman of the new Engauge enterprise he is partnering with Halyard Capital to build a next-generation **iDirect** and **iBrand** agency model.

6-Time Author

When *MaxiMarketing*, co-authored with Tom Collins, was published in 1986, David Ogilvy said: "Everyone in advertising must read this book." Ogilvy's comment started the authors on the way to bestseller stardom. Over 250,000 copies of *MaxiMarketing* were sold worldwide in more than a dozen languages. Five books followed, each with fresh insight into the turnaround from mass marketing to a revolutionary one-to-one paradigm first predicted a generation ago in *MaxiMarketing*. Rapp's new book, *Reinventing Interactive and Direct Marketing*, is sponsored by the Engauge agency in association with the Direct Marketing Association.

Keynote Speaker

Stan Rapp has been the keynoter at business conferences in just about every first-world country and in many emerging markets, including engagements at the Marketing Society of the UK, the American Chamber of Commerce in Tokyo, the Advertising Club of Bombay, the Marketing Expo in Sao Paulo, Brazil, the Europay MasterCard Members Meeting in Seville, Spain, the Australian Direct Marketing Association in Sydney, and in the United States at a wide range of industry verticals. He has had a role as keynoter at the DMA Annual Conference more often than any other direct marketing luminary.

Honors

Stan Rapp is a globally recognized marketing pioneer and thought leader. He was elected to the Hall of Fame of the U.S. Direct Marketing Association and was the first American admitted to the Freedom of the City of London as a Freeman of the British "Worshipful Company of Marketors." He is the 2005 winner of the prestigious DMEF Vision Award which has been given only twice in this decade. *Advertising Age* magazine, with the Advertising Club of New York, named him as one of the 101 "stars" that shaped the history of advertising in the twentieth century. *Investors Business Daily* featured his life story on its inspiring and widely followed "Leaders & Success" page.